To All My Children:
This Is My Father's World

To All My Children:
This Is My Father's World

by

JAMES R. MILLS

Order this book online at www.trafford.com
or email orders@trafford.com

Most Trafford titles are also available at major online book retailers.

Printed in the United States of America.

ISBN: 978-1-4269-5914-1 (sc)

Trafford rev. 03/01/2011

 www.trafford.com

North America & international
toll-free: 1 888 232 4444 (USA & Canada)
phone: 250 383 6864 ♦ fax: 812 355 4082

To My Wife Susan

Thank you for all the hours you spent on the computer to make this book possible. I thank you and God will bless you for your work.

To Our Children

God has truly blessed us with Christian children: Laura, Amy, Brenna, Rayna, Jason and Erin. Thank each one of you for help, support and encouragement.

To Our Grandchildren

God has blessed our family in many ways and many times. We pray that you will continue to follow Him throughout your life.

Britney, Pam, Kristina, Ashley, Joshua, Courtly, Shane, Micah, Sierra, Joel, Noah, Brandon, Cole, Austin, Ruth, Hannah, Ainslee, Brianna, Jake, Sarah, Hunter, Heath, Kara, Bradley, Oren, Chloe, Reagan, Jess, Ella, Darius, Seth, Lawson, Rachel, Hadley, and others to come

A special thanks

To my mother, Mildred Mills, for the cover design and to Erin Mills Ellis for her computer enhancement.

Table of Contents

Introduction

Well it seems that we are only to live on this earth a few numbered years. When I'm 75 years old, I'd like to make a video for you grandkids of me saddling up Bo, "swinging" up into the saddle and riding around the pasture. I would also like to make a video of me challenging you grandkids to see if I can still do the most push-ups. <u>But most of all I'd like to leave something that could help you kids and grandkids get through life and the upcoming difficult "last days" with more confidence, determination, and a closer walk with God.</u> I pray you will never lower your spiritual standards and that you will always know that, <u>THIS IS MY FATHER'S WORLD!!!</u>

Let's take a quick glance at the Bible and its purpose. Can I say in simple terms, that the Old Testament is to show God's never ending love and care for His people? The Israelites followed God some, quit and went to idols, were often punished by worldly kingdoms, humiliated, rescued and then free again to worship their God.

The Old Testament shows that sometimes God's people were worse than you can ever imagine–yet, He loved them and provided great things for them. The Old Testament is an example of the past so that you will have confidence in that same God to take you through the future.

Nothing I say should take away from or contradict the Bible, but rather add meaning to life as we travel through this world. I believe that God wants to help us in this lifetime if we'll let him. The Old Testament tells us what God did in the past. We see that He has absolute power over this world and His love and leadership were always available to the people!

Most of the New Testament is about Jesus coming to this world to show God's love, to provide a path for us to follow and teach us God's way. New Testament writers talk about living in the present time in this world and about God's forgiveness (example: John 3:16). They write, "come to me and I will give you rest" (Matt. 11:28). Characteristics we should develop, "the greatest is Love" (1Corinthians 13:13).

Then a little of the Bible is on the future, "...great street of the city was of pure gold..." (Rev 21:21). "I go to prepare a place for you" (John 14:2).

Therefore most of the Bible teaching is for NOW and about living in this world. That is why I try to emphasize and teach about living TODAY.

Remember when God created the perfect world? He walked and talked with Adam and Eve—He would like to do that with us too if we would let him.

Susan and I are very fortunate to have such wonderful, Christian children. Your Christian values and faithful habits are observable in your children's lives. All the things we do, and all the things we have in this world will soon be gone and when I dwell in heaven with Jesus these things will have been long since forgotten–but the things that really matter will never be lost or forgotten and every day I plan to walk past the throne of God and say, "Thank you, so very much that my wife and children and grandchildren will also dwell with you forever and ever!" All that really matters in this world is that each of us is preparing for eternity. We should walk in complete confidence that:

This is my Father's World!!!!

I would like to suggest a definite routine of study as you go through this book.

1. Find a time when you can be alone and not rushed. Also I'd like to ask you to seek and practice allowing God to answer your prayers in some way.

2. Do one chapter at a time. If they are small chapters you may do two. That may mean one subject a day so you can <u>think about it</u> occasionally. (ok fess up, most of you will read the book in one sitting) You are encouraged to do the chapter over again until you feel you have gained everything possible at this time–then go to the next.

3. Read through the chapter for understanding–As you read the chapter; try to understand what is being said. Don't think whether you agree or disagree (that is next) but just try to understand what is being said. Then use the blank paper at the end of the chapter to jot down "first impressions", things you agree with, things you disagree with, and reminders to review at a later time. As you read this I want you to keep in mind that the Bible is our final authority. (2Tim 3:16) "All scripture is God-breathed and useful for teaching, rebuking, correcting and training in righteousness."

4. FOCUS!!! FOCUS!!! FOCUS!!! I used to say things like "clear your mind, get rid of things in your mind and then think about Jesus." Actually, you probably can't just clear or empty your mind–your brain is always running and thinking of something. SO don't worry about getting all your daily stress out of your mind.

BE STILL and just start focusing on God or Jesus. Just start praising God. Feel free to say prayers out loud, sing songs, quote verses–let it all run together as you FOCUS more and more on God our Father and things HE has done for you and/or someone you know. Sometimes I feel like I have to get my mind going 90 miles per hour focusing on God to "push" out all the worldly things happening to me. My mind has trouble thinking of things I need to do today while I am singing songs like "Just a Closer walk with Thee." So singing helps me focus. I hope you take a little time and get an understanding of the hierarchy or order and priority of God's world and Universe.

Why I Write

The Bible says God created the heavens and the earth Gen. 1:1. He made the world and covered it with water and trees and grass etc. He made everything. In Psalms 50:10 God says He owns the animals in the forest and the cattle on a thousand hills.
Jesus stopped a storm, healed the blind, and brought Lazarus back to life–Wow!! What a God!! WHAT A JESUS–MY LORD AND SAVIOR!!!! Jesus did this by just telling it to be done!

My job has always been very important to me. Perhaps it was too important–in a few years I plan to quit my job. Jobs may come and go–but my relationship with God and the room Jesus is preparing for me in heaven goes on and on forever!!

So I should be more serious about preparing for my room or mansion that I will be in for eternity than I am preparing for next months house payment. In reality I need both but I need to realize that one lasts forever. Since I am going to spend eternity with God and Jesus I need to spend more time and effort toward developing that relationship and understanding.

I've always known, but it is becoming more "real" to me as our family grows–the only thing I can take to heaven AND one of the biggest joys in heaven will be <u>YOU</u>, my loved ones!! Your relationship with God is becoming the most important thing on earth to Mom/Gma Susan and me. We plan to spend eternity with each of you!

As you know, I know that when I die I'll go to heaven because of my relationship with Jesus. Sometimes I think of bad things I've done or I've even written a few of the mistakes I've made in life–BUT NONE of them count—they've all been ERASED!!! It may be that most of the "good" things I've done in life don't count for anything either!! What counts is that I've asked God to LEAD ME in this life and I am trying to live for HIM…. I'M ON MY WAY TO HEAVEN!!!! That's reason enough for becoming a Christian cause I may die today or tomorrow–I <u>know</u> that day will come sooner or later.

OK - OK, I've got my death covered–BUT–there is much more! Since I became a Christian I'm eligible for the promises and concepts written in the Bible! God, Jesus, and the Holy Spirit will help me through this life and in my struggles to live in a world in which I am not spiritually comfortable or physically compatible.

Now days that's what I tend to think about and write about the most. How can I develop a closer daily/hourly/minute by minute walk with God? "In the beginning God created…." So God made a beautiful wonderful place for Adam and Eve to live. God wanted man to enjoy living in the beautiful garden. Then in the evening <u>God would walk and talk with them.</u> They probably talked about what they did all day and naming the animals. I can just almost hear Adam saying "Today I saw a big animal that was so funny–you could hardly tell the front or back end because it had a tail on both ends, ha ha, so I called it an elephant." Someone may have said something like, "Someday they will build a car like that where both ends are similar and call it a Volkswagen, ha ha and they all laughed." And life was perfect.

Now the world has changed and God dwells within us. This same all knowing, universe creating, all-powerful God, lives within me. God wants to walk and talk and help us in our everyday life (in good and bad) the same as he did Adam and Eve in as much as we let him! I believe God, Jesus, and Holy Spirit are directing me to write this to help me develop a closer relationship and help YOU too! The world is changing fast and I and YOU need to test everything and pray about everything before we accept or sort through all the ideas and beliefs that are going around. While you read you will see that I am not strongly denominational. I try not to judge people or programs too harshly or quickly that are different than mine. Remember that Jesus himself was a radical and terrible problem to the religious leaders of the time! Even today someone that does things differently may or may not be doing our God's work—we have to study the Bible and pray for the truth. Then a constant question seems to be whom do we support financially? Often there are no easy answers.

You will need to routinely judge (Job 34:4, Philippians 1:10) and evaluate church programs, church beliefs, and even class material or ideas taught by an individual because it is so very easy to stray away from Biblical beliefs to "my" beliefs. However, I believe we are not to judge another person's salvation—only their works.

Here is a question I have heard. "Could I skip church meetings on Sunday morning and go fishing sometimes (or something similar)? When I go fishing I feel close to God." I think an interactive study group may be the most important study but I think the Sunday sermon is also important to regularly motivate and encourage you as well as educate you and strengthen your relationship with God and each other. It is time we spend honoring and worshiping God and recognize how great He is. Church time is a time to get the world out of your mind and open your mind towards God. The Lord's Prayer starts out recognizing God and then "hallowed" praise and honor to God whose name is over everything on earth and heaven!! That's only one hour of singing praises, several "types" of prayers, offering so I can be a part of

God's work, and maybe communion to honor and remember what Jesus did for me. That's only one hour. How much time do we spend other than that each week? AND it's not just the sermon. Sometimes, while my eyes are toward heaven I may get answers to other prayers or ideas that I want to write down. Sometimes I feel like I want to get so close to God that I can almost see us walking in that Garden of Eden. Can't you sing "In the garden" and just feel yourself there?

So here's the question–did these things happen to you while fishing? When you finish fishing stop a few minutes and answer this. "Did you worship <u>God</u>–or the <u>fish</u>—or <u>nature</u>—or <u>yourself</u>??" The sunset is beautiful, but is it enough for me to study the sunset or should I go and search and seek to know the God who made the sunset?

We really can't afford to use up time trying to justify things we do—like fishing on Sunday morning, etc… We can't afford to be guessing what Jesus wants me to do in situations so that we are "good" people. We can't afford to be thinking we'll go to heaven and our future is secure when we live "good" lives, and help other people and give money to something good, like "cure for cancer" donations. We can't afford to make any guesses on things that affect our eternity!! We'd better take the time to study the Bible and pray and then listen quietly with an open heart.

This book was written over several years with some taken from my notes on earlier experiences. I'll mention it more in a later chapter. I strongly, strongly, recommend you keep notes of your experiences and studies, in your spiritual walk. You will speak bolder and you will walk with more confidence and you will pray with more peace and understanding if you are often reminded of the things God has already done for you.

This just happened today and I need to tell you–so I'll just add it on here. I got home from work just after 2:00 this morning in the middle of the night. I got a little sleep and went to Sunday school early so I'm tired today. The grandkids all left right after Sunday dinner so Susan and I went to town to run some errands and I started talking and told Susan I was feeling depressed.

I said, "I'm really having trouble–I'm getting to feel depressed and swamped! I'm trying to write a book of God's care for us to encourage our kids not to get discouraged because no matter how things seem, God is over everything and He wants to help us in our daily lives and not just have a heaven for us to go some time off in the future.

Susan said, "God has always taken care of us. God is faithful! What I "feel" does not affect that."

I replied, "It's just that I need to get some field work done right now before it rains. My big tractor is starting to have trouble–I'll run it for now but it may need 4 or 5 of my days to fix it when it quits. My little Ford 8N tractor–the water pump is worn out and fan is wobbling around and hitting the shrouds. I started to work on it and it will take more time than I thought. Then this morning I see that something is dragging under the rear of your car–looks like park brake cable or something. And I'm tired. And I still have to get busy and move that big diesel engine from a combine to my main tractor. And I have the house back yard all tore up where I'm trying to bring in dirt and level it up." And more and more.

Susan said, "God has always been faithful to us and taken care of us and He will continue. Remember when we had the car accident a few years ago. There had been wrecks there before– people had even been killed there. Our car was totaled out. But we were well protected and taken care of. I felt surrounded by peace and love. I was absolutely sure God was in control as it all happened!"

"Remember the time we were traveling from California to Kansas? We were in the middle of nowhere in western Nebraska and our rear axle broke and we were going about 55 MPH frontward and then 55 MPH backwards... We spun around several times, and came to rest on the side of the road. No one was hurt! The car was packed down. The girls were sitting on the boxes, no back seat belts in those days and I was holding Jason in the front. A guy came by and managed to get the car to his garage: He "just happened" to have an axle that fit and he worked until midnight putting it in. His wife fed us sandwiches and entertained the kids and us while we waited. (I wished we still had their name and address.)

God is faithful. He has always taken care of us and will continue no matter how we "feel."

Then we prayed and I felt better.

We went on home and it was starting to get dark with rain predicted for tomorrow. I decided to go ahead and put the car right rear up on a stand to look at the parking brake. I put the jack under the spring pad and jacked until the tire was maybe four inches off the ground. I grabbed a stand and slid under the rear of the car but the car body was too high to put the stand where I wanted it. But I looked around a little, the broken parts were forward of the axle. Now remember, I have worked on cars, pickups, 18 wheelers, special large trucks and air plane engines for over 45 years now and taught mechanics some of that time too. I have made safety a habit.

So I went around in front of the rear tire and crawled under the car. I got so curious looking at what was wrong that I slid right under the car without putting the stand in place yet. Then I realized I'd better get the stand under that body seam. It was a tight fit so I wiggled the stand and barely got the edge of the stand under the body seam and there was a bang! The jack slipped and the tire came down on the ground and the stand held so the car body did not come down on me. In my 45 years this was probably my only jack/stand accident. I always slide the stand under before I get under–except this time. I am convinced that God allowed this to happen within His total control to get my attention.

Now tonight I feel more at peace. I still have to fix the car and tractors and a dozen other things; but I feel confident things will work out. God takes care of us!! Our family is so blessed!!!!

I've told you these things to show you what this book is about. Partly it's about mistakes I've made but my God has made things right!! I want you to know, that you know, that God is with each of you TODAY—or rather that EACH OF YOU IS WITH GOD TODAY!! He will help you walk through this world we live in!

You don't have to be really, really good–you just have to develop that special relationship with Jesus! I'm just an old farm boy that realized God was working in my life. The more I would "seek and search"–the more God would draw me to Himself. Our Heavenly Father wants to walk and talk with us, to teach us things, and to take care of us. My God made this earth (and all that is on it) for us.

My wife, Susan, is probably the best "Bible believe'n" and "Bible live'n" woman I know. She's just simple. When the Bible said God created everything in six days that means that God made everything in six days! We've seen God answer prayers for her many times! (I don't have a Ferrari yet though!)

We would love to see each of you walk with God and know that YOU are in HIS WORLD and that you are HIS CHILDREN! Walk boldly because this God that spoke the universe into being is in YOU and He loves YOU! I pray that most of all you will see God as an everyday God who wants to help you live better every day. Remember…

This is my Father's World!!!!

Believing & Faith

CHAPTER 1

There is a big difference between believing and faith. I have said that I believe in Jesus with all the belief I am capable of thinking. But, I want you to understand that Satan believes in Jesus more than I am capable!!! When you read Matthew chapter 4 it talks about Jesus going out into the desert 40 days and fasting. Look at verse 3 where Satan says, "IF you are the Son of God"—and then again in verse 6 he says, "IF you are the Son of God"—and we read that Jesus and Satan talk to each other face to face. My "believing" is limited until the day I can talk to Jesus face to face. While you are there look at verse 9. Notice that this time Satan does NOT say, "IF you are the Son of God"—because Satan knows to whom he is speaking. Satan believes and he knows that he is facing the true Son of God and he had already decided that he did not want to go a step further and follow Jesus in Faith. When we come to a point in our lives that we stop saying "IF you are the Son of God"–and we humble ourselves and say "Jesus, I need you in my life as my Savior and Lord of my Life"–then we begin moving forward in faith! (You see, Satan could not or would not humble himself at Jesus feet. Satan "believes" BUT he refused to turn that belief into action [faith].)

I could sit beside a river and "believe" there are fish in the river until I starve to death. Or I could throw a line, hook, and bait into the river and believe there are fish in the river and <u>act in faith</u> to catch one (faith is an action word to me!). Please allow me to interpret, with you, James 2:20-22, "You foolish man, do you want evidence that faith without deeds is useless (or dead)? Was not our ancestor Abraham considered righteous for what he <u>DID</u> when he offered his son Isaac on the altar? You see that his faith and his actions were working together, and his <u>faith was made complete by what he DID</u>." <u>So</u> then, our <u>actions</u> begin as you pick up your Bible and read it and you go to church and you begin telling other people and you put your money into the offering plate and you commit some of your time <u>doing</u> things as God leads you. <u>Many people believe there is a God but fewer people are willing and desiring to walk by faith and obedience and make God the head of their lives</u>!!

My favorite meaning of faith is in a story I heard many years ago. It seems that a man stretched a cable across the top of Niagara Falls. A large crowd gathered as he tightened the cable up nice and tight. The man was very careful to make sure the cable was just right. He jumped on it and took a few steps on it balancing himself very well.

Then the man asked the crowd, "How many of you <u>believe</u> I can walk across the falls on this cable?" The crowd had seen how professionally he had prepared the cable and how lightly he had taken a few steps on it. He seemed very capable so they all raised their hands.

Then the man got a wheelbarrow and asked the crowd how many believed he could push the wheelbarrow across the falls. Again they all raised their hands.

The man then went to one individual and said, "Get into the wheel barrow." That is where <u>believing becomes</u> "<u>FAITH</u>"!!!

When you first came to Jesus you believed he was a person who had walked this earth–history could confirm that Jesus was a living person. You learn to believe in Jesus. Then you may hear Jesus say, "Get into the wheel barrow we have work to do." Get into the wheelbarrow–step out and act in faith–learn to walk everyday in faith that God will take care of you.

Truly walking by faith can, at times, seem to be a very scary thing, and most always challenging!! My theory is that if you get to a place that your spiritual life is smooth or comfortable for a while then watch out cause things aren't quite right or things are about to happen! We just read in Matthew where Jesus talked with Satan. Jesus knew that from now on Satan would be close by watching and waiting for Him to let down His guard. Many times the Pharisees try to disgrace Jesus before the crowds of people and once the crowds started to throw Him down a cliff but he walked away. Worse yet—Jesus knew that one of his 12 closest people would deny Him at His worst hours on the earth. He also knew another would betray Him to the chief priests (Matt. 26:14-16)! If Jesus is our example–I don't see very much "comfortable" in His life.

I think God wants me (and you) to be <u>one step beyond what we are capable of doing</u>–and that keeps a certain amount of tension in my life! You see if God gave me an easy assignment I'd do it on my own and pat myself on the back. He wants the difficult or impossible so that I <u>KNOW</u> that I have to rely on His help. Probably the hardest thing I've ever had to do was not military basic training, or challenging high school boys to push-ups, or working to break a horse–the hardest thing I've ever done may have been (as an adult) apologizing to a man that I believe was wrong and that was not friendly. But I believe with all my heart that God wanted me to do that or I would never have done it!

If you ever think life will be easy if you try to follow the very God that created this world and all that is in it–if you ever think that you will be totally protected from all harm if you follow the

God that made us and knew us before we were born–if you ever think life will be relaxing because you follow the God of peace and love–just sit down and read the New Testament!! Read what Paul's life was like, or any of the other people that believed Jesus was the Son of God and decided to live their lives in faith!! All of these people BELIEVED that <u>THIS IS MY FATHER'S WORLD</u> and then moved/acted in FAITH!!

My God has a large throne. He can sit on it as King of Kings and Lord of Lords. I think that Satan does NOT get a big throne to sit on. He gets a folding chair and sits over to the side and watches Jesus and knows that He is real. When YOU KNOW (believe) that Jesus is real you have two choices–go sit with Satan or start acting on that belief—**that is faith**.

I'd like to talk about "feelings" and "emotions" for a few minutes. Don't ever think that God is with you only when you feel fantastic. God is with you <u>all the time</u> that you allow Him to be with you. Don't just judge by your feelings.

Never judge your relationship with God on your emotions. Everyone try this experiment. Sit comfortably in your chair and show emotions and expressions as I name them. Let's start easy and look happy. Then look sad. Now look excited–now look normal. They'll get harder. Now–imagine you are living in a country with marshal law and a midnight curfew for adults. What emotions do you show?? Unsure? Because you've never experienced it! Likewise you cannot fully know and understand the peace of heaven until you have lived with Jesus. If you cannot fully understand the emotions and feelings of heaven you cannot judge your walk with Jesus based on just your emotions or feelings.

When you watch movies like "The Ten Commandments" you see Moses hold out his staff and the Red Sea is parted. Not only is it parted but also the movie shows the water backing up on both sides of the Israelites and going way high up. Try to imagine walking through the bed of the river with the wall of water on each side of you rising up to the sky; or at least going high enough that you know in your mind that if it turns loose that you will drown at once! The Israelites had to walk right through this. If you were nervous or scared this distance across the river would have seemed like an eternity.

God could have done it differently and just zapped them to sleep and then had them wake up on the other side of the river, but he didn't do that. THEY HAD TO WALK through the river bed and they had to do the walk in FAITH. (Here again we see faith is an <u>action word</u>!) They **believed** they could walk out into/ through the riverbed. They could stand there on the shore and **believe** with all their heart, as the Egyptian army killed each one of them (or took them back)–<u>OR</u>–they could turn that **believing into faith**–faith is the action of stepping out into the riverbed and actually walking!!! God prepared a way–they had to step out in faith!!! (God can/will/does prepare ways/things for us but we have to believe and then turn that belief into action and that action is faith.) They had to have faith that they were doing what God wanted them to do or at least faith that God would care for them better than the army that was coming after them!! They had to have some faith that God would take care of them as they traveled out into the unknown.

Unfortunately, they may not have walked the walk in faith very well. They probably had lots of fear because of Pharaohs' army that was closing in from behind and the Red Sea in front of them that was impossible to cross. Even if they could swim they could not take the sheep and chickens and animals that could not swim. Also Pharaohs' solders would have continued to chase them forever until the Israelites were all captured and returned to Egypt to continue to work. Their faith probably increased as they saw Moses raise his staff and then saw the water part as only a miracle of God could do! Maybe life is a little like that as we look around with fear as some of the worldly things that seem to be closing in on us–but remember to look at the past and the things God has done and rejoice as you look ahead in faith and walk forward trusting that the same God that Moses followed will provide a path for us too.

When we walk in faith we sometimes have to go out on a limb or even do some things that seem scary but that is what faith really means–doing what God wants you to do and being where he wants you to be whether you understand or not.

You may be called or told to do things that appear silly or stupid as you do them!! Sometimes God's way seems too simple and we think that it can't possibly work. That's some more of what I call "one step beyond what you are capable of doing." Now be honest, "How would you feel, about the third day, as you are walking around the outside of the city of Jericho and the people come to the walls and shout, "We see you are back today–didn't you get sunburned yesterday?" OR "Well you just keep walking– we're in here drinking iced tea and lemonade" OR "Hey, why don't you sell your shoes and get a horse. Ha Ha Ha!"

Honestly, God didn't need those people to walk around the city of Jericho! God wanted their complete attention and total obedience!! There may be, but I can't think of a time when God told the Israelites to practice and train harder as they prepared for war–but I do remember a time (Judges 7:4-8) when He said "There are too many warriors so take them down to the river to drink." God told Gideon to keep the 300 fighting men that lapped the water as they drank and to send everyone else home. I don't think God needed super highly trained soldiers in warrior uniforms–He needs highly trained and skilled praying men in warrior uniforms keenly attuned to God and His will. God wants an army big enough to do a good job in battle, but so small everyone will say, "That's impossible for only 300 men to have won the battle!!!"

Now read this several times and maybe write it on your hand. God wants to win battles or anything He does with everyone saying—"That's impossible!" He wants the 300 fighting men to give their praise to Him and not to themselves. Also, with everyone talking like that, you will be reinforced (in your mind) over and over again how God did it–there is no way you could have done it!!

Also, right after a miracle, or answer to prayer, I want you to understand that Satan will start working on you to deny it all. "Maybe it was luck or fate or maybe I misread it or it would have happened anyway, etc." People all around you saying things like "It was impossible," will help reinforce the memory of God's power without a doubt and help build up your faith.

God loves to do the things we would call impossible. When we think it's impossible, God is at work.

Let me clarify this–I could run look again, but I didn't see a Ferrari in our garage this morning. God does not give me everything I'd like to have in this world. God answers prayer–yes, no, wait, etc... God sees "the whole picture" and I sometimes can't see or understand even part of the picture.

A friend of mine had a young girl the same age as our youngest daughter. His daughter was severely injured in a car wreck many years ago. I was able to travel and sit with him in the hospital, but I felt worthless. I probably mumbled things like, "God is over everything." Having a daughter the same age–I felt terrible with him–but I know he felt much worse than I could imagine. I kept thinking that God knew exactly how my friend felt. What bothers me most is if someone says something like, "This is God's will." This was not God's will for this child!!

God created the heaven and earth as our temporary and permanent living places. God created the plants and animals so we would have plenty to eat. He created the earth in such a way that we would be speechless by its beauty. When everything was ready He created a beautiful garden where we would live and work and walk and talk with Him. This was God's will for us!!! He made us special–apart from all the other animals and angels!!! God knew this girl before she was born–he created this girl special. I believe that my God was her Heavenly Father and her creator. I believe Jesus felt as bad as her earthly father felt. I believe that Jesus died on the cross because He knew her and loved her even before she was born!! I believe that Jesus hurt as He watched this girl that He loved so much, depart from this world at such a young age!

I really can't explain all the bad or hurtful things that happen to us–I have to just ride in that wheel barrow wherever it takes me, to go in **faith** that God is ultimately in control. When this world ends—-we already know how it ends—every knee and every heart will be bowed before our God and King and Father.

The end times are already written and I know beyond any doubt; I live in faith that:

This is my Father's World!!!!

Notes

God Is —

CHAPTER 2

To all my loved ones, let me try to explain something of my idea of God, Jesus, and the Holy Spirit. When I try to write about what God has done, I see that God is always the same, but invariably different in various situations, I'll try to explain.

We've been to several air shows and have sometimes seen the F-15 fighter planes (used to see the F-4 fighters) fly past. I would take pictures with my old camera as they flew past. That plane is great! I love to watch it roll, bank, or just head straight up. But, it moves so fast I might get a picture of the plane tail or front end or a wing or some other parts of the plane. Fact is I have several pictures of airplane tails!

It's kind of like that–I try to give you a glimpse of what God is like and no matter how "fast" I am, I can only catch a very, very small glimpse of the characteristics of God.

Exodus 3 tells the story of Moses and the burning bush. God is telling Moses to go back to Egypt, round up the Israelites and lead them out of Egypt to the land flowing with milk and honey. The Israelites will be cautious and unbelieving, so Moses asked, "Who do I say sent me?" God said to Moses, "I AM WHO I AM.

This is what you are to say to the Israelites: 'I AM has sent me to you.'" When I was young, I did not understand this but now I see that to say any more would be misleading. To say God is the Creator of heaven and earth would be true but it would be very incomplete. To say that God is the Leader and Father of his people would be true, but would be very incomplete.

I can't just put God in a "box" and put "rules" or "methods" or "consistent consequences" or limitations on Him. I hope that you will see that God does great and good things for us. God is very "flexible" and answers our prayers in different ways to be the best way for us.

As I read over the various events written in this book I feel like I see a different God or Jesus working in each situation to do what is best for me at that time. Yet I know it is the same God, who works specifically, lovingly, caringly, powerfully, for my best in each individual situation. There is a special peace when you allow God to take control.

Spend some time just talking to God and listening. God and the Holy Spirit have given Gma Susan and Erin several songs–sometimes while Gma Susan is driving on trips. Probably because she relaxes, clears her mind of worldly problems, talks honest and casual with God and then <u>listens</u>. During part of her life she was too stressed or busy to take very much time to listen. Driving a distance by herself she has the time to listen–that is perhaps the most important and hardest part for us to do!

The Holy Spirit convicts us of sin and the need for forgiveness. If you feel the Holy Spirit bringing your improper actions to mind, then you are to repent of those sins. If you decide not to repent of those sins and change your ways, then you are choosing to do what you want to do or what you think is right above what the Holy Spirit of God wants you to do. You will soon harden your heart to the working of the Holy Spirit–and that is the unforgiveable sin.

Sometimes an individual may think things like "Why did God let this happen to me, I prayed for God's help and he did not help?" Probably this individual is referring to consequences that are a result of something they did.

Let's look at the thought a minute, if you are reading this you probably went to school so you will be able to relate to this story in some way. Let's say that Popeye is in the fifth grade and he does something that is unmistakably against the school rules. He is sent to the principal–Popeye prays but is still punished. Why? Because our choices and actions have consequences!! Nowhere does it say that God will remove all consequences from action we do.

The Holy Spirit interprets, helps us understand and teaches us what we should say. He is the Comforter who gives us joy and peace and so much more. When Jesus returned to the Father, the Holy Spirit was sent to dwell in us forever. The "Fruit of the Spirit" will be reflected from you as you mature with Him.

While I'm thinking of the air shows, do you remember when one plane would fly by (not too high off the ground), and a second plane would fly under it upside down? They would move across the skies as if they were "ONE", flying in perfect harmony and synchronized together! This reminds me of the relationship between God, Jesus and the Holy Spirit. Together they make the perfect team as they fly close together and in perfect harmony as "ONE entity" or "ONE body." Or just as the two fighter planes can separate off and go independently for a mission, Jesus, God, or the Holy Spirit can go independently for any missions! There are lots of examples, but one I think of is that Jesus "prayed" regularly (as an independent part of the Trinity) to God.

The three parts of the trinity each have their own mission and responsibilities. I think that we ignore the Holy Spirit and fail to acknowledge Him. I sometimes talk to the Holy Spirit. When Jesus left this world, He introduced the Holy Spirit as the one who is in us and with us. He will convict us of sin, if we will listen and trust Him. He often teaches us and helps us to understand the Bible etc. and gives us understanding according to what we need and where we are in our spiritual walk.

Be slow to judge people and their beliefs of who Jesus is or how they worship Him. I like the church I go to and I know some or all of the people have a little different idea of who Jesus is. My "picture" or "ideas" of Jesus are based on my experiences and my studies of Jesus.

I was sitting in a church building once waiting for service to start. I looked at the large stain glass window with lots of divided colored "cells." Each of the cells had a different name of Jesus i.e. Teacher, Savior, Shepherd, Lord, and on and on. Although the cells were different colors and titled differently, there did not seem to be a major or outstanding divider between them. I recognized that Jesus is different to each of us. I would "call" or "name" Jesus according to my experiences and learning. For example, the person who knows that Jesus healed them would have a different "image" of Jesus, and pray differently, than someone who has not been healed. This is a good thing. Another example, a person that had experienced a healing might feel like making a career in medicine or make a ministry of visiting and praying for patients in hospitals (Hospital Pastor).

My experiences are different (each of us is different) and when you say "Jesus" I get a little different "image" than you do. However, we both worship the same Jesus. An example I use is my sister and I have the same Dad. When someone says "Dad" my sister and I have slightly different images that come to mind even though we are talking about the same Dad. Dad loved us both, but I see Dad as more of a disciplinarian than my sister does—maybe because I got more spankings than she did. I'm sure I was the better kid, but she told on me more. (It's funny how we remember the past.) Be slow to judge people that are different than us (from a different background), but worship the same Jesus. We are each different–we are supposed to be different–we are different parts to the same body (the body of believers [the Church]).

I was reading the colored cells in that large stained glass window: Healer, Master, Nazarene, Carpenter, Counselor, Prince of Peace, Friend, Living Word,… and I blinked and when I looked again the window actually had 2x4 (it looked like) boards as dividers of all the cells and a few larger wood beams that gave it strength. Also there were no names or titles on the glass—just the colored glass. We all believe a little differently and we each have a different job or position to fill. If we work close to everyone that has a desire to follow Jesus, then we can work together without 2x4's or any other restriction between us as we follow Jesus.

If you are old enough to remember, can you sing the song, "Turn Your Eyes upon Jesus" and look at how Peter started to sink in the water when he took his eyes off of Jesus. If you don't keep your eyes on Jesus or God, you will probably wander off track. When farming we see this example clearly. The easiest and straightest and simplest line to make across the field is the first one. My big field is almost ½ mile long. When I start out on that 1st trip or 1st round I just pick an object at the other end of the field and sight along the hood of the tractor (or something) to that object ½ mile away. You just drive to it! That goes very well and easy. Now, let's just say your implement is 20 or 30 feet wide. If you try to drive the second round while aligning yourself with the previous round worked and looking at the previous round right beside you, you will make mistakes. If you do the next round aligned from that previous round (2nd round) right beside you, you will probably make more mistakes. As you progress, across the field, you will be able to cover some of the previous mistakes, but you will make new mistakes. So–don't calculate or judge yourself or align yourself based on other people (right beside you)–align yourself with Jesus (right to the source)!!!

Let me explain what I mean by "align yourself with Jesus." First, let me explain the difference between a religion and a relationship. I sometimes use an example, my X, Y, Z & ME <u>Religion</u>.

Week after week the preacher or leader (X) is expected to study the religious material and presents a little of it in Sunday service. How well he presents the material depends on a lot of factors.

The Sunday class teacher (Y) works a lot of hours to make ends meet; so he doesn't have much time to read the material. So he gets his knowledge from the preacher or leader, mostly during Sunday service. His knowledge is limited and second hand.

Later, after Sunday class, let's say my wife explains it all to me. She may have a very limited knowledge of what the preacher told the Sunday class teacher who <u>then told</u> her so she could explain or interpret to me. She separates what I need or need not know.

Based on the information I am getting, I plan to direct my life into eternity. I'll follow the rituals of our church as we go through our Sunday service, etc… Rituals and rules make a good religion.

A <u>relationship</u> is based on a different purpose. Although my church service follows a scheduled bulletin, I am not bound by tradition, rituals and rules. I can communicate directly with MY Father God. When Jesus was on the cross the temple inner curtain to the Holy of Holies was torn from the top to the bottom. We can talk directly to God now without needing a rope around us to pull us back out in an emergency. I serve a Savior that came back from the tomb to help me and to take me into heaven someday.

The X, Y, Z and Me religion is a humorist look at my life sometimes. I need to study the Bible more, and communicate with our Father more, to build that loving and caring relationship first hand.

I am dedicated to serving the true living God because He has proven Himself over and over in my life.

My dedication to Him is a choice that I hope to choose to make every day and in each situation because I know:

This is My Father's World!!!!

P.S. Oh, have I mentioned lately–if you are ever bored in life you need to take a close evaluation of your relationship with Jesus and your prayer life! God will keep you moving one step beyond what you are capable of doing! You'll be amazed at what God (not yourself) can do! God <u>WILL</u> cure boredom, if you let Him work in your heart and life!!!!

Notes

My Father's World

CHAPTER 3

One of the most difficult times in my life was when I was going to the university (52 miles away) and you kids were in school. I could not do the roll of father and student and husband all at the same time and I was having a very difficult time. Finally, one morning I was driving to school and praying about all my worldly problems and neglects and things that were going bad–when I saw something I'll never forget. I know I've told you before but I really want to emphasize how very very important this is–especially as the world gets worse and worse nearing the end times.

I saw myself speaking in front of a church gathering and I call Jason to come up on the platform. I have Jason stand and I say, "Let's take a look at Jason's world AND let's see who or what is over Jason's world."

"Jason, let me borrow your billfold. If you look into someone's billfold or purse you get an idea of what their world is like."(I changed the items Jason had in his billfold to be his current life.) "Let's take a look–ok we see some money." I take out a few dollars and lay them on the floor between Jason's feet. "Money is important in everyone's world and is very important in Jason's life if he is going to survive and provide for his family and etc. etc... Here's a picture of Jason's wife–I know that Nichola is a very important part of his life so I'll lay the picture here between his feet. Next I see pictures of Jason's kids and I know they are precious to him and he spends a lot more time with these kids than the average Dad. I'll lay their pictures here too. I see a credit card–they are handy, especially if you are traveling. I see a membership card to a local gun club and shooting range– these can be for fun and relaxation. This driver's license can be absolutely necessary to get to work or go out for fun. Also I see craftsman tool club card—tools are necessary at your job and tools can be needed at home to maintain things that you own."

"These things represent Jason's world. Not everything of course, but some of the things in his world. As you can see his world is very diverse—some things are more for his occupation or job so that he can afford to live and enjoy life. Other things go more towards enjoyment and relaxation. And most of all Jason's world contains people that he shares his life with."

"Now let me ask you–who is over Jason's world? Jason is, of course. Right here you see Jason standing over his world."

"But wait: let me look again–who/what is over Jason's world? Let me back up a little and try to get a look at the whole picture. The ceiling is over Jason's world! Well then the building roof must be over Jason's world too. The sky and the clouds would be over Jason's world too! The God who made heaven and earth and is everywhere must be over Jason's world also!!"

"So when we take a look at items that make up Jason's world and lay them at his feet it is obvious that Jason is over his world. Jason has a lot of control over his world. It is also obvious that the ceiling and roof are over his world but they have no control or no value in his world. Then if you believe there is a God who made everything and that God is everywhere and that God is over everything then you can understand why I say THIS IS MY FATHER'S WORLD."

"Remember I said that Jason has a lot of control over his world. If I believe that this God exists (and I do) then this omnipotent God that is totally over Jason's world would/could have some control over Jason's world. Look at this "picture" now, Jason's world is just a very small pile here that is covered by this large ceiling, roof, sky, and clouds and this huge God that made all, knows all, sees all, knows the past, knows the future, loves us all, and knew us before we were even born–can you see that this Heavenly Father is over all your problems and cares!!!! Satan runs around this world right now BUT our God is still the ultimate power over this world!!!! I may be directly above my problems but my God is above me–so my God is over <u>MY</u> problems, cares, and concerns. My God is bigger than all my PROBLEMS!!! Therefore, THIS IS MY FATHER'S WORLD!"

Jason's world does not look very big laying here at his feet. I know God cares about Jason's world and every detail is important. This God that spoke the stars into existence, carved the Grand Canyon with His hand and puts life into every baby born can handle Jason's every problem AND my problems AND yours!!

Now I know that looks can often be deceiving and sometimes it is hard to see that: but, I have to live and walk in faith that God is over all. I cannot live by "feelings" but rather I am called to live by "faith". Seek and search and ask this Heavenly Father–this all-knowing God to take control of your life and be the shield over your world. I need to learn—<u>DON'T LOOK DOWN</u> AT MY PROBLEMS BUT <u>LOOK UP</u> AT A GOD THAT IS OVER ALL MY WORLD!!!!

I believe that God lives in me; do you believe that God lives in you?? Do you know what that means? This God that created the world is in me! The King of Kings is in me! I am powerful!

I have this God that owns large herds of cattle in me! I have the God that made the mountains which contain lots of gold and diamonds in me! I am rich!

I have the God that Jesus prayed to in me! Jesus died on the cross for me—because He loved me! I am loved and reborn!!

I believe that I am a much loved, powerful, confident person to the degree that I can turn my life over and live for Him! I believe I am a most blessed person— Susan and I have six children and 34 (today's count) grandchildren that are blessed with very few health problems and a love for our God.

It may not always "feel like it" (don't rely on feelings). But,

This is My Father's World!!!!

Notes

Living in God's Will

CHAPTER 4

Maybe the oldest question of time or the most often asked question is, "How do I know God's will?" Well, one verse in the New Testament says something like "Be you transformed in your minds that you will know the will of God." So, the first thing is that your mind must be transformed so you do not think like this world, but look upon God and His ways all the time. Not easy. Definitely it takes consistent and constant dedication that I am incapable of doing, but God takes the impossible and I don't give up.

If we are going to talk about God's will, we need to go back to the beginning. God created the heavens and the earth and everything therein, and it was GOOD. I want you to understand this–read Genesis 1:1 THROUGH VERSE 25. As God created the earth and sky and heaven and all the animals and everything in those 5 days–God saw that it was GOOD!

Then on the sixth day God created Man and Genesis 1:31 says: "...it was <u>VERY</u> GOOD"!!

Why did the wording change in verse 31?? It changed because in the first five days God was just making things in preparation for the real final product. The ultimate creation— Adam and Eve then YOU and ME!! Genesis 1:1 says: "In the beginning God created the heaven and the earth." In the beginning of what? In the beginning of this time period we might call "man" or "man and the universe" or "man on the earth." Try to think about forever and ever as a long period of time for right now. Then we could take a look at just a small portion of that as the time man has existed on earth. We could look at this period of time as the "Time of Earth and the unknown (Heaven or Hell)" if we were real scientists??? Or we might call this period of time "Man and his Creator" if we were sociologists??? This period of time starts in Genesis 1:1 when God created the heavens and the earth.

The Bible shows that for five days, God created the individual parts of the earth or universe. Each part was GOOD. So, the main creation/attraction was yet to come! The earth, as we know it, was created as a home—a temporary place for man to live. Just as I believe that Jesus went to the cross for me–and that He would have gone for me alone, I believe God would have created the earth for me and that He knew ME before I was born (Jeremiah 1:5).

Let me take a minute and go back before Genesis 1:1 and the creation of the heavens and the earth. There was the Trinity—God the Father, Jesus the Son, and the Holy Spirit. What did they do? Maybe they threw comets or something across the universe and got points for the black hole they hit–oops there was no universe before Gen 1:1 so it can't be anything like that. Maybe they supervised the angels—that sounds about as boring as trying to play chess with me. Without us people things sound boring. It is hard to imagine "things" for them to do. I think they "communicated." For example, Genesis 1:26 they were talking to each other, "Let us make man in our own image." They communicated with each other.

There are angels, but they lack a lot. The angels were made to be very, very good and may not have shown things like a "need" for God. They may have automatically obeyed, etc. For example, imagine your young child comes to you and says, "Daddy will you help me put on my shoes?" Unless it is one of those days–you experience special joy and feelings that your child comes to <u>you</u>. Also, it is special that he or she "needs" you. We like to feel wanted and needed. I think God wants us to ask Him for things, and help, and even for our every day food and drink. God wants us to be His children!! He is full of joy when we go to Him and want to communicate.

Let's see if I can explain something. I love my wife, Susan, and I love my 6 children and they are very special to me. I love my 34 grandkids (that's today's count) and each is special and I enjoy the individuality I see in each one. They are each born or adopted into our family–and family is a special bond to us. There is another girl, Regan, whom I have a special love for too. I was sitting in church one time and a little girl came in, walked down my pew, climbed on my lap and has called me Grandpa ever since! Regan makes me feel chosen, like a god… I never made things occur so she would want to communicate with me–she chose to be special without even knowing or realizing that was happening. I think God feels chosen and excited and the angels rejoice when each one (yes, each ONE) of us accepts Him into our lives!!! How could we talk about God's will without understanding the things that God loves? Looking at what Jesus loved is fairly easy–He loved people–He loved children. Jesus was all about people…

God loves every time that we go to Him–especially when we just want to talk and share our lives and be willing to talk and listen (communication). God made us to communicate with Him and to worship and praise Him. To live as His special people, close to Him and in harmony with Him **because we want to**.

Now, let's go back to the creation and God said it is GOOD. Then when He created man He said it is VERY GOOD, because man was the ultimate creation that the earth had been made for.

Then in Gen 2:15 God put the man in the Garden of Eden–WHY–to work and take care of it. God did not say He and the man would take care of it–He told the man to take care of it. Then God made a helper to help the man (woman).

Gen. 3:8 talks about how God came walking in the cool of the day and I believe God wants to share things with man and communicate. God <u>walked</u> and <u>talked</u> with man! In the beginning things were designed or led to the purpose of God and man talking and sharing. I believe that God would like to share all the secrets of the universe with us–but we could not handle information like that. Also notice that God continued to talk with Adam and Eve even after they were put out of the garden. God even talked to Cain after he killed his brother, Abel.

God also created man to praise and worship Him in all things and at all times. The Bible says we are to praise His name forever. One song writer said "Turn your eyes upon Jesus". He is our leader and protector.

Please **stop** here and **read** Psalms 44:1-8. I think these verses are beautiful. David said, "Our fathers have told us what you did in their days." David is saying that actual events guide his knowledge of the power of God and what He can do today!! "I cannot trust in my bow, my sword does not bring me victory; but you give us victory over our enemies, you put our adversaries to shame."

Acknowledging and recognizing what God has done, and **therefore what he can do**—the people are believing and know they need to live constantly and consistently in God's will, if they are to be under God's protection and leadership. Life here is getting extremely complicated. Has God's acceptable will or plans for man changed? Not at all! It takes the time and effort of searching and seeking and knocking to get to "know" God.

Well, I stumbled there about the definition of "God's will." God's original and perfect will was that Adam and Eve would live in the garden in peace with God. That failed. God allowed man to strive to live by laws/rules that God would accept with various sacrifices."

Then in Gen. 3:16-19, God told Eve the consequences from her eating the fruit and God told Adam the consequences of his eating from that tree also. Then in Gen. 3:21, "The Lord God made garments of skin for Adam and his wife and clothed them." In other words God told them they disobeyed and fell short of the perfect life they had been given. BUT, that He still loved them and He made garments for them because He would still be their God and care for them. Notice that they already had clothes–in Gen. 3:7 they had sewed fig leaves together for clothes. BUT <u>God wanted them to have better</u> so He made them clothes of skin.

Two things here… One is that Adam and Eve made their clothes of leaves because they had never killed an animal. They had probably never thought of it!! God killed an animal here for man's use. Animals and all creation are here for man's use–not abuse but for our use. Second, that by making them the best clothes, God is saying I am still your God–you are still my people–and I will always care about you.

We are to live in God's acceptable will. I can't live in God's original plan (His perfect will) in the garden, BUT, I can live as close as possible to living the plan God has for me now.

Remember that you were originally designed with the natural ability and desire to walk and talk with God in perfect peace and relationship. You were designed to live in a beautiful garden with flowing rivers and tasty foods where even the animals lived in harmony with each other.

Think of that–we still walk this life beside the God that made the heavens and the earth!! I walk constantly beside the God that said, "Let there be light," and there was light as He began this amazing creation. I walk beside the God that convinced Egypt's pharaoh to let the Israelite slaves go free and then led the people <u>through</u> the Red Sea! I walk beside the God that knocked down the walls of Jericho and led His people into the Promised Land!!

Is there anything my God, which I stand beside, can't do?? I need to live in true faith and search and seek and strive to get closer to my God so that I can learn to walk with Him and listen and know His will for me. Read the Bible. This God that did all these things for His people wants to take care of you and me. Can you hear this God in some way saying, "TRY ME"? I think this God that created all things says "Try me in your everyday life and try me in the small things so that you can build up faith to try me on the bigger things. You are my children and your problems are my problems and your decisions are my decisions too."

Gma Susan and I are often praying about what to do or which way to go. God has answered our prayers in several different ways. Sometimes God does something great (like a promotion) that I'm not expecting. It's difficult to explain but when I receive a special "happening" that is an answer to prayer, I'll probably see (in my mind) a previous time when I was praying for answers. I receive this answer with unbelievable peace and joy. In other words sometimes God answers our prayers with what we call miracles or answers to prayer. To be sure we recognize them He will show me a "flashback" of a time I was praying for this answer, so that I unmistakably identify the answer with the original prayer. There may even be a few months between the original prayer and the answer.

There have been times—usually in my prayer time I will get a flash in my mind like: "wait." Kids, there are a lot of things I wish I could explain to you! More than anything I want that each of you would be so close to God that you can walk and communicate with Him daily!!!! Let me try—when I am thinking it is usually slow and sometimes I think back and forth. When God puts thoughts into my mind it is rather quickly. So the whole thought may only be a fraction of a second. Also, when God speaks it is matter-of-fact and with authority.

Sometimes I think there is no answer—probably I just fail to see it and maybe it's a negative answer.

I should be the best to walk and talk and praise God continually after my experiences—But I fail a lot and am pulled by the world.

Definitely my biggest handicap is myself!!! The best thing is God's forgiveness and grace!!!

Ro. 12:2, "---be transformed by the renewing of your mind...," James 4:8, "Come near to God and He will come near to you...," Put the world aside and concentrate on God and His ways. Keep an open mind and talk to God. He wants to communicate with you and provide for your needs.

I often say that my Bible study and prayers center about "living in this world" and getting through life here. What was Jesus' life about?? Don't just look at the cross and the "temporary" end of His life. Jesus spoke a little of "going to prepare a place for you" but His life was about teaching us and showing us how to live. Example: One time Jesus healed a blind man (Mark 10:46-52). Jesus asked the man, "What do you <u>want</u>," NOT what he <u>needed</u>. The man <u>wanted</u> to see and Jesus healed him and made his life here on earth so much better. We sometimes get hung up whether things are needs or just wants–Jesus did not debate the difference—He often took care of both. He cared and He made life better here on earth!!! Another example: Jesus' first recorded miracle of making the wine had nothing to do with life eternal but made life here on earth much better at the time and who could resist their mother?

The famous story where Jesus fed the 5,000 people was the same way–it just made life easier/better for people. There were times when Jesus did miracles for people and told them not to tell. He made life much better for those people by healing them even at the risk of conflict with the Pharisees and gathering large crowds earlier in His career than He wanted.

Yes, Jesus was here to lead people and prepare them for heaven–and to train His 12 replacements. But His life was about

LOVE and SERVICE and TEACHING to make life better here on earth. That is my goal–whether speaking to a crowd or giving some encouragement to someone I meet I'd like to be able to make life a little better for others. The promise of heaven is great and wonderful but that's a long way off. I try to study and prepare to live for today. Sometimes this world seems cold and cruel but always remember:

This is My Father's World

Notes

COMMUNICATE

CHAPTER 5

In late 1986 I did a children's sermon that I'd like to repeat for you now. I reminded the congregation that we had been living in Italy and one of the BIGGEST things we missed (besides relatives) was McDonalds or Wendy's or Hardy's and all the others!! So, when we arrived on the east coast we got ourselves organized and then went to the closest fast food place to eat. (This is a standard ritual for people returning to the U.S. after a tour overseas of several years.)

Since we are a big family we usually split up–I take some of the kids and go find the biggest table and Susan gets in line and does the ordering. After a little while she brought the food over and we passed it out and everyone looked it over to see if it is what he or she wanted–and you would not believe it!!! Mine did not have miracle whip on it. Susan and I had been married 20 years!! She had fixed my meals and been with me half of my life; yet, she had failed to put miracle whip on my sandwich. Maybe it was the excitement of being back in the United States or maybe the excitement of being back in the world of fast food shops, and surely it was the excitement of getting to go see our relatives again soon! Whatever the reason it was hard for me to imagine because I was so sure she knew me better and knew what I would have wanted.

Later when I thought about the whole situation I decided that God our Father wants us to know Him so well that we would know at least some of what He likes and dislikes. I really believe there are a lot of things God would like us to know about Him if we would sit still, listen and take the time to study and seek Him. To build a close relationship takes lots of time and caring effort. It's not always easy, but I should strive to build a relationship so close that I'd know what God expects even in time of heavy stress or fast moving excitement. At the same time remember that our God wants us to communicate with Him and talk with Him about everything and every decision we'll make. He wants to be a part of our everyday lives!

This is the same with marriages. Most couples would have a much better marriage if they communicated more or better. Communicate with respect towards the other person. There is an old story that goes something like this: The husband is leaning on the driver's door as he drives the car down the highway. The wife is day dreaming as she leans on the passenger side door. Rather slowly she says, "Remember how we used to sit close together and you would put your arm around me and hold me while you drove?" The husband looked over towards her and said, "Dear it isn't me that has moved."

God hasn't moved! God was with me and probably talked with me before I was born… God was with me when I was much younger than today. I did all of the talking then but as I look back I know that God was a part of my life. These days I see that my God is still with me–He hasn't moved. I know He cares. It's me that can't sit still and listen to Him very well.

God created the perfect Garden of Eden and walked and talked (**communicated**) with Adam and Eve.

I think that before this world was made the Trinity just **communicated** with themselves and the angels.

We say that prayer is communication, but is it??? Almost all prayer is us talking. Once in a while we talk AND listen--that is verbal communication. We think of verbal being the only form of communication but that is not true. A lot of our communication is not verbal but rather we "act out" what we think or believe. Let me add here: if you have children around, one of the best "communications" is us adults saying the meal prayers. First, it is you thanking God for the meal (you talking) which shows you are thanking God for the daily things (as shown in the Lord's Prayer). Second, it is non-verbal action (stop what you're doing and hold hands before you eat) that will set a good solid memory for the children.

While I'm thinking of children–kids are really great at reminding me to say things like the meal prayers until the things become habit. Grandkids and Gma Susan worked together to learn Bible verses!! A small Bible study with a couple little kids can be a learning experience.

I think the Trinity still communicates a lot. Seems like Jesus prayed/talked to God often. I wonder what they say about you. I wonder what they say about ME.

Does our non-verbal communication reflect that Jesus will be coming soon?? Does our verbal communication tell other people that Jesus will soon be coming???

No matter how things happen in the future always remember that:

This is my Father's World!!!!

P.S. We took a trip that went through Hot Springs, Arkansas. I casually remarked that someone needed to wash up the statues because they were dirty.

One of our grandchildren, Courtly, (about 5 years old then) said "That is really bad." We questioned her "what is really bad?"

She answered very seriously, "the Bible says not to 'wash up' statues."

Finally we realized what she was saying and I carefully explained the difference between "wash up" and "worship."

God will bless the children extra because they can accept what they hear and love Jesus without trying to change Him. Read Matthew 18:1-6 and Mark 10:13-16.

Notes

Be Availuable

CHAPTER 6

You are called to be <u>availuable</u>! That's all one word "availuable". I often think that one of the most important characteristic us servants of Christ should have is to be "available." Then we need to be "valuable" when we get to our mission place. We are to live a life where we are listening and in tune with Jesus so that we are able to go wherever and whenever He wanted us to go. That is a valuable characteristic of a Christian. Here when I talk about go anywhere and anytime, I am not really talking about other countries. I'm comfortable with the idea that God got this job for me, so I'm talking about going to someone down the aisle or next to me. It may be words of encouragement for someone or a word of praise. I think God puts ideas in my head–like go visit someone in the hospital or other things around here. I could give you success stories, but I will tell you about one guy who got out of the hospital and was home for a while. God would put him on my mind–that I should go visit him.

I was busy on the farm, he had physical therapy, or they would be gone a while.

We did a good job of avoiding each other. Then I heard–he had started drinking. He confessed to God and his church and is doing ok now. My Point?? This did not happen to him over night. The sad part is he is not alone! I am part of the blame! I believe God put him on my mind so I would go visit him. Maybe, if I'd gone the Holy Spirit would have given me something to say. I should have tried harder. All of us men suffer if one of us fails! We should always be a family/team!

God doesn't really need my money–He has "the cattle on a thousand hills" (Psalms 50:10). Then why do we take an offering? God works through people. By working through people, it gives us an opportunity to be a part of God's work. That may be missionaries or local ministries. Also when we give to the offering we are reminded that all we have is God's. When we joyfully give some back to God, it reminds us that all is His. (Communion reminds me that I am God's, and I offer myself to him as He gave Himself on the cross for me.)

The first recorded miracle Jesus did was to turn water into wine. One of the most famous miracles was Jesus feeding the 5,000 people fish and bread. Jesus didn't need money to meet the everyday needs of food. Read Matthew 17:24 where Jesus and his followers were being charged a temple tax. Did Jesus need money to pay taxes? NO. Jesus told Peter to go catch a fish–take the money from the fish's mouth and go pay the tax. Jesus did not need my money for special expenses of this world. He could get money anywhere–even from a fish's mouth!

He doesn't NEED just one more person (me) to go to heaven because there are lots of people He could take if He just wanted numbers. God wants someone who is willing to move this way or that way when He says and do what He says!

I am also coming to the idea that God wants you to be "valuable" when you get there. Available plus valuable equals (availuable.) That does not mean valuable with money or jewelry or fame or popularity. It means that you have a desire to do God's will, an increasing knowledge of His word, and a longing to be at peace with God and to hear His voice. When a soldier is sent somewhere he has value only in as much as he has the ability to represent his commander and do what he is supposed to do. When we are sent to do a task, no matter how large or how small, we have value only in as much as we have the <u>God given ability</u> to represent our Commander and King and do the task that we are supposed to do!

Let's just take a look at that famous (famous for the wrong thing) man named Jonah. Oops; as this story starts out we see Jonah is NOT available! It seems that Jonah is saying to himself <u>something like</u>, "No way, I'm not going to Nineveh. I don't have time for those people, I'm busy, and besides I don't care what happens to them, and they deserve whatever they get!" It seems that God bothered Jonah some more so Jonah left town in another direction to avoid God and his assignment! Well Jonah had a few really rough days, but when the fish coughed him up onto the dry land Jonah decided that he had time and he was available to go do what God wanted!! It also seems like Jonah was valuable when he got there. He must have done exactly what he was supposed to do—even though he hated to do it—and God's plan was accomplished and the city of people repented and was spared from destruction.

We need to be in constant training so we can be <u>availuable</u>! That means we'll be <u>available</u> for any of God's assignments or missions and <u>valuable</u> when we get there so that God can work through us to accomplish His work.

"Available" means that we are tuned in on God's radio beam like an airplane following the beam as it flies towards its next goal. It doesn't stray to the left or the right. "Available" means we are so in tune with our Lord and Savior that we are willing to drop what we are doing and do what he wants us to do.

"Valuable" means that when we are where God wants us to be we are willing to put <u>ourselves aside</u> to do as God wants us to. In our weakness He is made strong. In II Corinthians 12:9 Jesus says, "My grace is sufficient for you, for my power is made perfect in weakness." Valuable means that we can put the world aside and let God work a miracle through us! I can only plant a seed by what I do or say–the Holy Spirit then has to work in their or my life. Just like Jonah finally was valuable to God's mission in Nineveh. Jonah simply told the people what God wanted him to say (he was a valuable worker for God). Jonah was probably not even enthusiastic or excited or happy about being there or helping those people!! Or he may have been overjoyed to tell them that God was going to destroy them!! He may have talked in a dry monotone, unhappy voice and the people may have been able to see that he did not want to be there–but they listened and God moved their hearts! Take up your cross and follow me includes the burdens and love and helpful actions that you share/ do for others. He was valuable because he did exactly what God told him to do. Then he sat back and waited for God to destroy those terrible people that didn't deserve to live upon this earth. BUT, the Holy Spirit worked in the hearts of the people and they repented and changed their lives!!! They were spared from being destroyed.

Being availuable means living in harmony and staying in tune with God. I am reminded of that song about turning your radio on. Our inner radio is supposed to always be on and tuned to Jesus.

Sometimes God told the people where to go i.e. Jonah, Noah, and others. Sometimes God led the people. Exodus 13:21 "…. the Lord went ahead of them in a pillar of cloud to guide them …."

In Exodus the Israelites were leaving Egypt after being slaves and in bondage and they were going free! They were going to the Promised Land where they thought everything would be wonderful and they'd live happily ever after. After being slaves the Promised Land sounded like heaven! Now all they had to do was follow this cloud and it would take them to a wonderful peace, happiness beyond words, and maybe riches and fortunes for everyone!

How about you? Have you ever followed a cloud that would take you to a promised land? What or who was in that cloud? Was it drugs, alcohol, belief in yourself or friends? Or was it the Lord??? Did the Israelites really believe the Lord was in that cloud or were they so excited about "freedom" and "not being a slave" and about how they were getting themselves out of Egypt that they quickly forgot that the Lord was in that cloud and that <u>He</u> was going to lead the people? The Lord is the way to the Promised Land and only He can lead you there!

We must be going <u>towards</u> something and not just running <u>from</u> something. The Israelites had a choice. They could be running AWAY FROM the <u>PAST</u> slavery in Egypt that was a strong negative in their minds. Or, they could be running TOWARD the <u>FUTURE</u> in the Promised Land and all the positive things they are expecting.

Keep your eyes on Jesus wherever He may go. Acts 1:9-10a. "….he (Jesus) was taken up before their very eyes, and a cloud hid him from their sight. They were looking intently up into the sky as he was going…."

This is my Father's World!!!

Notes

Submission

CHAPTER 7

One of the biggest problems in our world today is "submission." When you mention the word "submissive" some people think "oh yeah, I know about that. That word is used where it says (women are to be submissive to their husbands)." (Ex. Col. 3:18) People sometimes imagine a negative scene where the wife (usually) is ruled by a domineering and physically abusive spouse. That is not the picture I see as I read the Bible! The main idea of those verses is NOT just directed at women.

Sometimes I hear things like "I can't be nice to that person," or "I refuse to talk to that person or stand beside them or whatever" or "there is no way I will ever be submissive to that person, UNLESS they are really nice to me first." STOP my loved ones— REMEMBER–Jesus went to the cross for YOU and ME! I was not even born yet–I had not done anything nice to Jesus. Then I was born and grew up doing some bad and evil things–I had trouble doing anything good–BUT Jesus was nice to me–I did not deserve anything whatsoever good–BUT Jesus was nice to me–I put myself first, and I neglected God in a lot of ways–BUT Jesus was nice to me and He went willingly to the cross and gave His life up to be "nice" to me (and you)!!

I'm not talking about you being nice to someone first and then they may like you back and even submit to you–I'm not talking about being submissive to some domineering person or dictator!! I'm saying we (especially me) need to stop this super paced world we live in and say "Jesus, I love you. I believe–I realize–I KNOW that you died on the cross for me and that you paid for (you were the living sacrifice for) my sins before I was even old enough to have sinned! I want to live in submission to you."

I know it can be tough being nice to someone who is not very nice to us first. Jesus walked on this earth before us. He KNOWS what it is like trying to be nice or submissive to someone who is not even nice back. In (Matt. 20:27) Jesus said we have to be a servant or slave!! Jesus said "the least among you will be first." (Luke 9:48) Jesus also said, we have to be as little children if we want to go to heaven.

So I tell you–we have to pay attention to Jesus who was willing to go to the cross when we were not worth saving. We have to pay attention to Jesus who was willing to love us and prepare a way for us. We have to be submissive–we have to give allegiance–we have to show obedience to, we have to love and trust Jesus who died on the cross to prepare a path and a plan for us to survive and an eternal heaven for us to go to!! And all the time He knew that we could never do anything to deserve it. We can do something–we can submit ourselves to Jesus and God our Father and strive to live in a personal relationship with them.

Read James chapter 4. In Verse 6 "… God opposes the proud, but gives grace to the humble." Verse 7 "Submit yourselves therefore to God."

When writers like James talk about submission they are talking to each of us and our personal individual relationship with God and Jesus. This <u>word</u> does not differentiate between male and female or young or old or race or past experiences or rich or poor or level of education.

The word "submission" should bring up positive thoughts where each of us is praising and worshiping our God and Creator. These thoughts should be focused around God's awesome, everlasting, and unconditional LOVE for us.

Jesus did NOT say "I am your Master and you will submit yourselves to me at all times." Jesus did NOT say, "If you always do things my way I will take care of you." Instead Jesus said (I summarized and reworded), "If you love me, If you love and take care of each other, If you have the wholesome, pure, total love of a child, I will go and prepare a place for you, and I will send the Holy Spirit to dwell in you and guide you and teach you, and be in you to help you on your voyage through life." Jesus wants us to submit to Him so that he can give us—and so that we can receive— the "good life". We have to want, we have to seek, and strive for a life of grace and peace and love. We need to be submissive to God so that He can fill us with these "Good Things". There cannot be two masters in us (ourselves versus God). Because if "ourselves" wins—we lose! "Myself" gives into sin and selfishness, therefore life is better when I submit to God and allow Him to work good things in my life.

The word "submission" is about living our life in a close relationship with God and a strong desire to always do God's will. We should have an invisible shield around us with God's Love and Peace flowing from us. 1 Peter 2:13 "Submit yourselves for the Lord's sake to every authority instituted among men." Hebrews 13:17 "Obey your leaders and submit to their authority."

"Children, (Col. 3:20) obey your parents in everything, for this pleases the Lord." "Father's do not cause your children to stumble. " Eph 6:4

We can understand that submission is about our <u>personal</u> relationship with Jesus and our desire must be to put Him first in our lives and be willing to live for Him.

Submission also refers to our willingness and ability to recognize and live by God's chain of command or lines of authority. (Ephesians 5:22-25) talks about the lines of authority in a Christ centered family. (James 4:7-10) Means there is only ONE way a man can fulfill his leadership role in the family–that is to become totally submissive to God. I believe a good leader is a great follower–say that again–I believe a <u>good</u> leader is a <u>great</u> follower–and he must be following the right God and be submissive to that God. Then to be a Christian Bible believing wife, she needs to learn to be submissive to her totally submissive Christian husband. Then there will be harmony.

When the husband is in place it is easier for the wife to get lined up with and in submission with her husband so there will be harmony. Human nature can quickly wreck the whole program! Notice that this harmony of a Christ centered family starts with the husband!!! ALL MEN should study the Bible and know the role that YOU are to fill in the family!! We are to love our wives as Christ loved the church (the bride) when He went willingly to the cross. YOU CANNOT TAKE THAT LIGHTLY!!!!! That is a huge responsibility!! First to your wives and then to your children!! Look at Jesus as the example:

1. He set an <u>EXAMPLE</u> that was so perfect and righteous that He could say, "Follow Me."

2. Jesus set <u>RULES</u> that were to be followed. He told His family (the church) to "Love one another and Love your neighbor as yourself." Jesus made rules to help us all live in harmony and peace. Men, do we make rules in our families and do we make them for that reason alone?

3. Jesus (as the husband of the bride) made <u>GUIDELINES</u> that promoted harmony and peace and comfort and a true gentle love!!

Read Matthew 11:28-30 where Jesus said to come to Him and He would give us rest, for He is gentle and humble of heart.

4. Jesus <u>PREPARED</u> a future for the bride!! John 14:2 & 3 says He will go and prepare a place for us (in heaven) and then He will come back and get us.

<u>HUSBANDS ARE YOU THERE</u>?????? That is your responsibility and you <u>cannot</u> delegate your duties away. Think of all that includes!! It's scary. Men we need to align ourselves with the Bible teachings and live submissive lives to our God. The aligning of all the family is on our shoulders.

Wives, ideally, when the husband is aligned with the Bible and is submissive to God–THEN–you are to be submissive to him and God. Matthew 6:24 says that no one can serve two masters. I would also say to you that two masters cannot serve one family. Soon there will be a "tie." In Genesis 2:18 God said, "....I will make a helper suitable for him (Adam)." God did not say slave or anything like that–He said a helper. Ephesians 5:22-33 talks about the relationship between a husband and wife same as the relationship between Christ and the church. I could never say it as beautiful as it is said in those verses.

This is not about who is boss or who cleans the house–it is about having/showing respect and love (love is: 1 Corinthians 13:1-13). Ephesians 5:22-33 just sets the rules so there is no fighting over the roles each person serves.

The submissive husband is lead by God and is training in the Bible. The Bible believing, Christ centered wife will then submit to her God fearing husband. Then there will be harmony.

That goes against the very principles of our society. Our society teaches us early in life to get first place, always win, be top dog, and fear no one. Later, in some jobs you learn to "fight" to get ahead, or "step" on people that get in your way. Then you understand the Bible to say that we are to submit ourselves to God—but we are not taught how to submit and humble ourselves!

Then think about Jesus telling Peter, "If you love me feed my sheep." That is a very peaceful, loving, caring thought.

Think about that a minute—sheep may be one of the dumbest animals. When I was very young my Dad had sheep. I remember one field where the sheep would stick their heads through the woven fence wire and then be stuck. In the evening I had to help them get their heads out of the fence–it seemed like the same sheep day after day. It seemed like they could not learn! Never! Are people the same way?? Read the Old Testament–watch people you know–as a last resort look at yourself–do I make the same mistakes over & over??? Think of how "dumb" I look to God!!! I've trained dogs and I've trained horses and I've watched trained pigs; BUT I have never seen a trained sheep! Jesus was telling Peter to humble himself enough that he could submit and wash the feet of His <u>sheep</u>. Jesus was telling Peter to be a servant to the people and to be caring and thoughtful enough to meet the needs of the people. Jesus was telling Peter to show love even to the people who act like sheep—without condemning them.

How can we become a Christian except that we humble ourselves before God, acknowledge Him as all knowing and all powerful, and give up our own pride and ego to submit ourselves to His will?

There is an unforgivable sin that comes from hardening of the heart or refusing to listen to the Holy Spirit. It comes from believing we are right and refusing to humble ourselves and submit to the God who created everything! It's a terrible thing to lose eternity because we refuse to establish that relationship and submit to our God.

Another thing society teaches us is that if a person is born different, or with fewer abilities, or on the "wrong side of the tracks", then that person is worthless or of less value. But the Old Testament is clearly a story of a people that often gradually turned away from God. They worshiped idols; they completely neglected God's ways to the point that the people seemed almost worthless for any use. Yet, God would take care of His people. God loved them (and us) enough that He sent His son to the earth to be humiliated and discouraged and tortured and then hung on a cross to die.

Because God made each one of us and because each of us is/ has a valuable part in God's work here on earth, we should never feel like a loser. We are winners on God's team if we will submit ourselves to Him and try to live in His will–more so than our own!

Let's see what the Bible says about submission & marriage. Both husband & wife are to be submissive, James 4:7 "Submit yourselves, then, to God." Ephesians 5:21 says "Submit to one another out of reverence for Christ." Wives, Eph 5:22, "Wives submit to your husbands as to the lord", Col. 3:18, Wives, submit to your husbands as is fitting in the Lord".

God created man and woman to love (a word with many meanings 1 Cor. 13) each other in marriage. Not for one to be a servant–but that both should serve and help and complement each other. In Genesis 2:18, God created woman to be a helpmate. Marriage is about combining the dreams and beliefs and goals of a man and a woman into one combined effort to make this world a better place for you and your growing family. To encourage each other, to seek the Lord daily and help each other turn the problems and joys of this world over to Jesus. Pray together consistently and share your inner thoughts and feelings so that you can support and understand each other and be in agreement before the Lord. Ephesians 4:26 says not to let the sun go down upon your wrath and come to an understanding that you can agree to before the Lord.

Certainly, sexual experiences are a part of marriage and they should bring the couple close together. Let me see if I can split this up a little. These verses "tell it like it should be" and our lives do not always go in the proper ways. You sometimes see the drawing of the triangle and it says God, husband, and wife at the three points. Suppose the husband chooses not to be in harmony with God and takes himself out of this triangle. The wife needs to love her husband and be faithful and submissive to him unless the husband wants her to do something that will harm her continued relationship with God.

Everyone's first line of obedience and submission is to our eternal God—the rest (or anyone else) comes after we establish and continue our relationship with our God. This applies to husbands, wives, the boss at work, and everyone in authority or leadership. This applies to our local church too. Our Pastor Dean LaVelle is a man close to God's heart. As my spiritual leader–God put him in that position and Pastor Dean is careful to bring honor to God and himself. I submit to him in that position but, I must watch and judge that he does not cause me to damage my relationship or my submission to God and His will. We have to be alert at all times and in all things. Ultimately "I" am responsible for what I do. Pastor Dean can teach, counsel me–even yell at me—BUT—I am responsible to verify if his words are right and true, before I do things.

I was tremendously fortunate and blessed to have married your mother/Gma. She was often the stabilizing one of our family. She insisted that Sunday school and Church were always important. She made sure that prayers were important.

We live out in the country and there are several one lane bridges around here. If two cars come at the bridge from opposite directions one of them will have to yield or be submissive. Marriage is like this bridge. When two people (married) come at a situation or a question from opposite sides–one of them must have the final word. In as much as possible they should discuss, carefully listen, and treat each other with respect. More than likely they will come to a mutual understanding and agreement. If necessary the man, as head of the house, will have the final word. (I often say that I will make the final decision as soon as my wife tells me what to say.) Our marriage is made up of two individuals. Very rarely would we make a decision that does not affect both of us. Depending on the seriousness of the decision, we should be willing to spend time in discussion and <u>prayer together</u>.

I feel certain that all of you grandkids will get married someday so I'd like to leave you with a few things to consider. First of all I'd really, really hope and pray that you marry a true Christian. I have heard the comment, "After we are married I'll convince my spouse to become a Christian." Let's think about that a minute– people sometimes change or move toward the way that is the easiest. Let's say, for example, you get up on Sunday mornings and get around and go to church while your spouse would sleep and then go out for brunch and have fun. If you are not a strong Christian, it is possible that you would start drifting toward your spouses' way of life! Since sleeping late is the easier thing to drift toward unless you really hold your values. Eliminate a bunch of temptations and frustrations by carefully selecting a Christian to date and to share your life with. God instituted marriage for you two to "**CARE AND SHARE**" your lives together–intertwined and interlocked so that you become one. An important part of your marriage should be, <u>caring</u> for your spouse and truly wanting the best for him/her and <u>sharing</u> your spiritual insights, knowledge, understanding and enthusiasm to support and encourage your spouse in all they do as you both live and walk with God.

Can you imagine not having someone with you to say "Amen or Yes, Yes" when you get excited about something and say "Praise the Lord?" But rather have someone with you that says, "You're crazy or dumb"?? I am reminded of the Bible verse 2 Cor. 6:14 &15: "Do not be yoked together with unbelievers…" I'm reluctant to admit it but it seems like the ways of the world, and not the will of God usually wins out and is the easiest way to go. I usually think of this as marriage–but it also means close friends and partners in all matters of this world. Sooner or later the two, or more, of you will pull or drag the other one along.

Deut. 22:10 says do not yoke an ox and a donkey together... If the animals are going to get the work done properly, you need two animals that have similar abilities and interests. I am more familiar with horses and mules as dissimilar animals. Several years ago my Dad bought a very nice mule. My Dad and the mule are getting older and don't want to run and jump or play so much anymore. Well, one time I rode my horse and Jason rode Dad's mule and we started across country and came to a small creek bank. My horse ran a little and jumped upon the bank–the mule walked up to the bank and stopped and (I'll better tell you mule's have coil springs made into their hooves!) that mule just sprung up and onto the bank! Can you imagine what would happen if a horse and a mule were harnessed together and trying to pull a wagon of kids through these fast paced lives we live? If you are a parent in that family your wagon is probably going to crash and your kids may be scattered. I may be closed-minded, but I can't imagine a life with someone who does not share the same basic ideas of religion. I often ask Gma Susan things like, "What does this Bible verse mean to you??" The devotion and dedication to a common religion helps cement your relationship into a common unity.

Perhaps the second thing in your marriage should be your willingness to give yourself to your spouse. This can be risky and may make you feel very vulnerable but I think it is important that you and your spouse give of you inner beings. For example, I do not want to expose my inner feelings (??), to people I work with by saying something like "I'm scared of spiders" or I might find rubber (hopefully rubber) spiders in my tool box drawers the next week. However, I should tell my spouse all kinds of things about myself so that my spouse can understand me better. If my spouse cares about me, then this kind of information would be received in a caring manner.

Marry a good friend. This seems so simple (??); maybe I should not even mention it. But think for a minute; maybe you will be spending 50, 60, or 70 years together. When you get up every morning and sit down at the breakfast table wouldn't you like the person you see in front of you to be your best friend?? Let's say that you are going to take a trip for a week, wouldn't you like the person you will be spending all that time with to be your best friend??

Obviously your marriage will not be perfect. Soon after Gma Susan and I got married we moved to northern Japan. I often say our marriage is so good because we learned how to fight! There wasn't anywhere to run off to so we learned to argue and fight and then get over it rather quickly. I've heard of people that wouldn't talk to each other for days or where one of them went back home, etc, etc. Those are days that are wasted or lost forever. But if the truth ever gets out–Susan and I are probably still successfully married because people prayed! We came from parents that pray.

I cornered Kristina one day, and I "suggested" she marry someone that will make a terrific Grandpa. Plan for the future. The years will go by fast and you'll soon be there!

I've already mentioned that you should care and share but there will still be times that you get into strong disagreements. Don't be alarmed–all couples that quickly change to mate and match their life styles and habits <u>will have</u> disagreements and strong confrontations!! The question is not "will you fight" but rather "how will you make up"? The Bible says don't let the sun go down on your wrath. In other words, end the fights quickly; don't let them drag on for days and days.

Susan and I often enjoy talking about how married couples divide up the work. This will change as they have children that accept more and more responsibilities while they mature. A few years ago when Gma Susan and I were just married we had a neighbor lady that always mowed their yard. Gma Susan said she did not want to have to mow—that was a good thing because I wanted the outside jobs. Gradually through the years we shuffled jobs and responsibilities around sometimes swapping jobs to fit our needs. Sometimes Gma Susan helps outside and I empty the dishwasher and help with the laundry. We often help back and forth. We have both had a turn (several times) at writing checks, paying bills, and keeping track of them. We are pretty good at talking (communication) back and forth. We know couples where she pays the bills and they do not communicate. For example, if the bank account gets low, she may pay some bills via credit card. Then she might decide not to tell him so he won't get stressed. Now as head of the family he can't make good sound decisions. Essentially she has usurped (grabbed) his responsibility.

Wives, who usurped her husband's responsibility, did things like this to protect her husband from stress. To make good decisions on any subject, he needs good information. When he starts making bad decisions he loses self-esteem and self-confidence as leader of the family.

Communication is one of the most important parts in the glue of a strong marriage. One of Gma Susan's favorite jokes is about the 3 hard- of- hearing ladies who went for a ride on the upper deck of a double deck bus. The first lady said, "It sure is windy up here." The second one said, "It's not Wednesday, it's Thursday." The third one said "I'm thirsty too, let's get off." Marriage should have lots of communication with humor, love, and acceptance of each other.

Wives—your husband cannot be head of the family and pray properly and make good decisions if you cause him to fail. All the facts! Dragnet was an old radio show where Detective Friday would say "the facts ma'am, **just the facts**."

I've often heard that "Life isn't fair!" This applies to marriage and a lot of other things. But tell me, how would you feel if you were dragged out in front of a large crowd that kept yelling, "We'll

kill you in the electric chair and let Wichita BTK killer go free?!"
The crowd wants to kill you when you have not done anything
wrong and they are willing to let a guilty threat to society go free.
I would agree with you that life is not fair–but Jesus, who was
innocent of any crimes or sins, stood quietly by and let them put
him on the cross until he died, while Barabbas went free.

"Life isn't Fair" could have been the main discussion by the
loved ones when Lazarus died because Jesus was not there to
protect him. Even if people were thinking that, they would have
quickly changed from that negative attitude when they saw Jesus
and Lazarus talking and walking together again later. Life may not
have seemed fair but Jesus came and changed those attitudes. So
when you get those feelings that "Life is not Fair" just remember
that Jesus is not done yet. We may not even notice what happens
later on but always remember, **"GOD'S FAMILY WILL WIN"**
(that's us!). My Dad's favorite song and one that I love to sing is
"I'm so glad I'm a part of the family of God." Gma Susan sings a
song about "Jesus never fails" and I want you to never forget that!
When you start to feel low and that life isn't fair I want you to stop
and remember that you are on the winning team. Your marriage
and your family can be on that winning team. The end times are
already written and in those days God will conquer all evil and
those that walk in faith that Jesus is the Son of God will enjoy
eternity. How would you like to be on a soccer team or basketball
team that knows with complete certainty, that your team will
become the champions even before the games begin?

As time goes on it will get more difficult to live a Christian
life, but remember "NO MATTER WHAT HAPPENS KEEP YOUR
EYES ON JESUS". Try not to spend time watching other people
and the things of this world because those things will drag you
down, and change your mind to useless negative thoughts! Instead
strive to fill your mind with things from the Bible, prayers (both
talking and listening) and things that are good.

"Finally brethren, whatsoever things are true, whatsoever thing are honest, whatsoever things are just, whatsoever things are pure, whatsoever things are lovely, whatsoever things are of good report, if there be any virtue or if there be any praise think on these things." Philippians 4:8

"For the rest, brethren, whatever is true, whatever is worthy of reverence and is honorable and seemly, whatever is just, whatever is pure, whatever is lovely and lovable, whatever is kind and winsome and gracious, if there is anything worthy of praise, think on and weigh and take account of these things—fix your minds on them." Amplified version.

This is my Father's World!!!!

Notes

JWDYWMTD

CHAPTER 8

To all my children, read this carefully and be sure you understand what I'm saying before you comment on it, please. I'd like you to focus your mind on God and then read with an open truth–seeking–mind and heart. Remember that I want you to challenge and test and pray about EVERY idea before you accept or reject the idea. We people have a habit of accepting or rejecting things too quickly because they sound "good" or "right" or "religious."

The letters WWJD (What Would Jesus Do?) have become famous over the last several years. A while back I really felt the Holy Spirit was trying to tell me something about this and finally I caught the message. The letters WWJD have left out the most important thing--we are supposed to be asking JWDYWMTD (Jesus, What Do You Want <u>Me</u> To Do) in my daily life and/or in this situation!!!

It is an important thing to get to know Jesus as well as possible and by keeping a close personal relationship you will be forming opinions and understandings on what Jesus would do in various situations. I wish that each of us could form a relationship that close. However, it is not really, really important that we analyze what Jesus would do in a given situation–as it is extremely important that we find out what <u>we</u> are supposed to do in a given situation and then do it! Jesus had a life that He was supposed to live–He had a path that He was supposed to follow–He had a job that He was supposed to do–a destiny only He could fulfill. He lived that life to the point of perfection and I am so thankful that He did!

NOW, the question is, "Can I live the life that I'm supposed to live and do the things that I'm supposed to do??" When I get into situations will I do the right thing?? What is the "right thing" for <u>me</u> to do?? Have I walked with God long enough and close enough to know what He wants <u>me</u> to do in every situation? Have I studied God's word and prayed enough and listened enough to know beyond a doubt what He wants <u>me</u> to do in every situation?

Let's look at the prayer that Jesus left as an example, "…give us this day our daily bread …." Why did Jesus say that when it is so obvious that we need food every day? God wants to be so intertwined in our daily lives that we will know that He wants us to ask for and talk to Him about every little common thing–even the food that we eat every day. Take nothing for granted–but talk everything over with Him.

Even if I try my best I can not always become accurate about knowing what to do. Did Jesus leave any other examples that would help us to learn to become closer to God? As I read the Bible I see that Jesus prayed a lot and when He finished He prayed that God the Father's "will" be done. In every situation will I pray, "Jesus, what do you want me to do so that your will can be done?"

Someone told me that when I get in a "situation", I should ask WWJD. The answer to that would be–pray. So I should then pray what should I do. <u>OR</u> When I get into any "situation" I should pray JWDYWMTD.

Do you know the best thing (first thing) to do in any situation (good or bad)?? I Thessalonians 5:17 has only two words, "pray continually." Those two words must have been important if Paul set them aside as one verse instead of combining them into the rest of the sentence. I Peter 3:12a says, "For the eyes of the Lord are on the righteous and his ears are attentive to their prayer". Talk to God! Communication. We know that we will need food to eat today–God knows we will need food to eat today (and every day) but still Jesus said, "Give us today our daily bread." No matter how difficult or how common something is God wants us to:

1. Recognize Him as the supreme power and creator and provider of all things.
2. Communicate our every need with Him.
3. He wants us to look to Him for everything, not our government or the company we work for–although He may/will work through things like these.
4. He wants us to call Him "Father."

I am realizing, #1. God has a plan or a path for me to walk during my life here on earth and #2. I could never get to a point that I really understand our Omnipotent God. Therefore, I must learn to come to the point where I trust God and am obedient enough to ask "Jesus, What Do You Want Me to Do" in every situation of my daily life.

There is another point I'd like to make here. Our God wants us to be in constant communication with Him. God wants us to be His children, He wants us to talk and listen to Him constantly, He wants us to discuss our decisions with Him, He wants to tell us many, many things but not until we are ready and our relationship is how it should be. Would we be willing to listen? I would not listen to a God that I did not recognize as my God. If

Jesus spent time in prayer, <u>we should spend a lot more time than He did</u> in communication with our Heavenly Father whom we are trying to get to know and understand.

Someone may say that they want to keep WWJD because we are to strive to live like Jesus and that He was the perfect example. Yes, this is true, Jesus was the perfect example and yes, I will strive to live like Jesus. I believe one of the greatest examples that Jesus set for us is that he prayed a lot. Matt 14:23 & Luke 22:41&42 say, "Jesus went out to pray." Then he did what the Father wanted/expected Him to do. Matt 26:39 says "not my will but thine." If I am going to follow that example I need to be praying constantly and asking JWDYWMTD (God/Jesus, What Do You Want Me To Do)? In Matt 16:24 Jesus said, "If any man will come after me let him deny himself and take up <u>his</u> cross and follow me." Luke 9:23 "If any man will come after me, let him deny himself, take up <u>his</u> cross <u>daily</u> and follow me." Jesus wants me to pick up <u>MY</u> cross (that cross represents total dedication, total trust, total commitment, total devotion and unwavering love until the very end) and follow Him! JWDYWMTD

I could take that a little further. Let's say a person gets into a situation with several choices of things they could do; so they ask themselves WWJD? They may be able to pick the "right/good" answer without having a close relationship with Jesus–or May not even be a Christian. I have met people with very high morals and "good" values that could pick the "right/good" answer of what Jesus would do. Many non-Christians can do that. Therefore, being able to pick the answer to "What Would Jesus Do" does not say much about an individual. If you ask a group of people WWJD you may get the same answer—the answer that Jesus would have picked.

On the other hand, if a person were to get into a situation with several choices and ask JWDYWMTD (Jesus, what do you want me to do?) then you could know the proper direction to go. For example, God, our Father may want an individual to verbally witness to someone in the situation, or He may want an individual to do (action) something in particular, or He may want another individual to just leave the situation and the area. JWDYWMTD becomes a <u>personalized</u> question–a question that recognizes Jesus as my all–knowing leader and shepherd. It is a question that shows my submissiveness and my willingness and my desire to follow Jesus' way for <u>ME</u>.

The answer may not even be the one that you would choose or your favorite answer. Let me give an example. Our church had small church meetings on Sunday evenings. It was decided to try something new with classes or study groups instead. One class was directed toward men who wanted to become deacons or elders. Another class dealt with evidences of faith or modern miracles and answers to prayer. There was another class that was already full and then a childcare center that needed a few workers.

Right off I can tell you the one I would love–I get excited about modern miracles and things that God is doing TODAY in answer to prayer. But I was reluctant because that class was filling up with women only–many were wives of men in the other class. Susan would be helping in the childcare area so I decided to help in there if I did not decide where to go that first night.

I had not signed up for a class and so we were driving in to church that evening to watch the kids and I explained the whole situation to Susan. We prayed and then it was decided to continue as planed but with an open mind. For some reason, we agreed that if someone should come to me and ask me to join their class I would go to that class, and if nothing happened I would stay there and help watch the kids.

****Remember, have an open mind when you pray!! NOT easy sometimes! Be open minded and ready to accept **ANY ANSWER**. Why would you ever ask God a question and then limit the answer or not be willing to accept the answer. If you are going to live by your own "will" you will be disappointed and discouraged. (Go back to chapter 4 and reread about getting prayers answered.)

Sometimes you hear that God did not answer prayer–it may actually be that it was not the answer we wanted, so our mind would not accept the answer. At the end of our prayers we say "Not my will, but your will be done." Can we accept that when we say it??

Another thing about praying is to be specific. If you have a flat tire, pray that God will send someone that is very competent at changing tires and will change it quickly and safely. Now back to my story. ****

Try to imagine now, we get to the church and I walk down the hall and into a classroom that children are starting to gather in. The men's group is starting to form in the sanctuary at the opposite end of the building and the class of women that I'd like is in between. A guy just older than me walked into the room and I recognize that he seems out of place because he does not have any small children with him: but he invites me to come join the deacons and elders class. I try to sidestep the question because I'm hoping to get invited to the other class yet. But, he is persistent and says there are enough other people in there to watch the children, so why don't I go to class "with him."

Then I realized that is where God wanted me to go. At the time I'm not sure why, but I knew it was the thing I was supposed to do–so we immediately left to the men's class and that was the beginning of more adventures as a deacon.

Let me look at that "with him" above. Try not to send or tell people where to go or what to do—if possible take them. Walk that extra mile so people will feel like family or partners with you.

Summary: One of you may have made a note that WWJD or JWDYWMTD is getting picky. So let's look at that. The Jewish religion and possibly others have some physical parts to them, i.e. you may have been required to carry or lead some birds or a sheep/ram to the priest for offerings (not really hard but physical). Now Jesus made Christianity with our heart and soul and <u>mind</u>. Let's say that Christianity gets right down inside of you to your frame of <u>mind</u>!

God wants you to get into a "frame of mind" where you will "pray without ceasing" even for the food you get each day! You know that when building any house or mansion, the foundation must be built first. Then the house frame must be built and it must be "perfect" if the house built upon the frame is to be "perfect"!

Therefore, we have to get all the way into the "perfect" frame of mind if God is to build a "perfect" and beautiful home in us. I Corinthians 6:19a "Do you not know your body is a temple of the Holy Spirit, who is in you, whom you have received from God?"

Summary 2: Part of this JWDYWMTD has to do with obedience and commitment. After we ask and get an answer we are to <u>take that action</u>!! That action may make you "standout" in the crowd or make a spectacle of yourself! How do you think Daniel felt as he continued to worship God instead of the king—knowing that he would be thrown into the lions and that everyone was watching him? Sometimes in life we have to standout and stand for what God wants us to do, knowing that:

This is my Father's World!!!

Notes

God is My Pilot

CHAPTER 9

The Old Testament is close to being or actually is a <u>R</u>eligion. They lived with a bunch of <u>R</u>ules they were to follow. When they slipped up, and at various times of the year, they had a set of laws about which sacrifices they were to bring to the priest and exact things they were to do or not do.

When Jesus came He changed the "<u>R</u>" word to <u>Relationship</u>! That Relationship was centered between God and us—but it also included our relationship with each other. Jesus was the final live sacrifice and <u>external</u> Requirement!! Jesus said we are to worship Him <u>internally</u> with all our mind and heart and soul! For example, The Old Testament Rule said you could not physically harm another person—the New Testament was built around a Relationship with other people so that you would not even THINK (internal) of harming another person in any way!

Therefore, this new Relationship with God requires a new and different state of mind. Our God, the Alpha, is to be number ONE in our life. Our God is above everyone and all things, He made all things, He created us, He can easily stop our next breath–but He totally loves us, we are to be His children.

In one of the Chapters I talked about how pointless it is to try to live by feelings alone. Feelings can lead you astray. Some days you just have to choose to be and live a Christian life even if you don't really feel like it. How you say things can make a difference in how you think in your Christian life. What you think over and over will become "fact" to you.

Christianity is a mindset–WHEN WE CHOOSE to FOLLOW JESUS and GOD we must TOTALLY put THEM FIRST!! Following is an example.

Have you ever seen that bumper sticker that says, "Jesus is my copilot?" Let's think about that a minute. Doesn't that infer that you are in charge of your life and that Jesus is in the second place chair?

Maybe we should go around and ask people to tear up all those signs etc. that say God or Jesus is my co-pilot. Replace them with "God is my pilot," for until then, we are in trouble! For you see, the pilot lands and does the take offs. In times of bad weather and problems the pilot takes control. But when everything is calm and peaceful and there is little chance of trouble the pilot lets the co-pilot hold the controls (very simply stated!). On a larger plane they may set the auto-pilot. But if a decision is to be made the pilot makes it and assumes control. Is that the way we are to treat God? Do we let God hold the controls of our life if and when everything is easy and calm and we are "high above the mountain tops?" Do we let God lead us and take care of us when things are not easy and calm??

Maybe my problem is like going through pilot school. I'm finally getting a chance to pilot an airplane and my instructor will be beside me. While flying along we run into rough and shaky weather. I get worried and stressed and very nervous and I grab the yoke and clutch it in my hands very tightly. (While riding in a car high in the mountains and/or other stressful places I'd rather drive than be a passenger!!) I feel better if I can think I'm in control!!!!

Along that same line—it used to be that a pilot had to get a higher instrumentation rating to fly in bad weather. I don't know now days. It is harder than you think to fly by instruments. Let's say the gauge shows one wing higher and one lower, but you don't "feel like" you are at an angle. What do you do?

So, if I was learning to fly I'd have a lot of trouble giving up the controls to someone else—and sometimes I have trouble just giving my problems to God.

Maybe my problem is like going through pilot school and I'm in the class where I'm flying the airplane and I will need to flip the switch for the auto-pilot to take control and guide the plane. I get all excited and my adrenalin is flowing but after a little time I flip the switch and the auto pilot takes over. After a time I begin to relax and develop a peace and confidence—and all goes well and I feel contented until—until there is turbulence and then in my nervousness and fear I automatically and mechanically, without thought, grab the controls and take over! And I fight the autopilot and take over for surely I must drive when there are problems. Oh, I have to learn to not be controlled by "feelings" but to believe and trust and to live by Faith that the real pilot in my world is always my trusted Lord and Friend.

We can all relate to the compass. Have you ever been with someone that said, "That is north," and you said, "No, No, north is over there." OR Have you ever been somewhere and you just know for sure the compass is broken because north is supposed to be over there!!

It's the same way with flying or living, can you turn things completely over to God to lead you and be your pilot?? It is extremely difficult most of the time, BUT we have to learn to! For example, Jesus can't "lead" you to heaven if He is in the co-pilot seat of your life.

Jesus said, we can't have more than one master (Matthew 6:24). We have to decide which one will sit in the pilot's chair of our life. Jesus also said we can't be lukewarm (Revelation 3:16). That means we can't follow Jesus sometimes and ourselves alone sometimes.

That pilot's chair is "control" with some characteristics like supreme power, infinite love, creator of everything we see, total power over life and death, and much more!!!!

This is very difficult to live, but when you read over this, who should be in my pilot's chair?? In your life??

I need this bumper sticker stuck on my arm so I'll always see it, "God is my Pilot." You won't want anything less!!

How can I let God be in control of my life? Practice! Practice talking with God and following his directions in small matters, and later the big issues will be automatic. Also share with people and let them tell you things that God is doing and it will help build your faith.

NOTES:
1. Set your Compass by the Master.

    I have flown in small propeller planes a few times. I sit up front where I can see out good and where I can watch the controls and indicators. If I remember right, one of the first things we always do is set the compass.

    To set the compass we'd taxi out toward the runway and stop. The N, E, S, W, would be marked (usually painted on the pavement or concrete). For our own safety and peace of mind we'd carefully set the compass before we started to fly. We trusted those N, E, S, W. markings. Those markings have been correct and helped pilots in the past so we'll trust them with our future!!

    Let me change the subject. I sometimes hear things like, "I don't read the Old Testament–it's boring". Or maybe,

"All we need to read is the New Testament." I used to think things like that too. Now I see the Old Testament strengthens my faith, gives me confidence, and teaches me some repeatable history! The old master compass AND the God of the Old Testament were often tested and were always found to be true and dependable. Time after time God rescues His people. God will take care of us too if and when we stop and let Him! A future with God based on a past with God.

So align your inner spirit with God, Jesus, Holy Spirit, and the Bible so you can feel confident about your future that is based upon a proven past!

2. Be Like Jesus.

    Luke 22:42 Jesus "needed" and "wanted" an exact specific answer to his prayer! I'm sure He wanted to avoid the pain, the ridicule, the separation or alienation from God and people–He wanted to avoid this death on the cross BUT he was willing to do whatever God the Father said.

I want to be like Jesus–this does NOT mean (thank goodness) I have to walk five miles a day because Jesus may have averaged that many. It does NOT mean any of these or any other physical things. Let's look further–it does NOT mean I can turn water into wine or feed 5,000 people with just a few of Long John Silvers' fresh deep fried fish.

It refers to the very basic thread of my spirit! Let me explain— God made us in His image. Was that with long curly hair? OR a nice wooly beard? OR pretty blue eyes?? NO! NO! We are made in spirit like He is in the spirit!!

Now, if we are to be "Christ like" we must have our spirit lined up and in tune to God's spirit. Example: to be "Christ like" we must spend time communicating with our God like Jesus did.

The Bible says, "Jesus went up to pray as was His custom." That's not all—we must be willing to say "Not my will but your will be done."

Jesus probably did not say, "You have to communicate (2 way communication) with God our Father 22 minutes a day." He probably did not say much—but He lived as an example! Prayer was so important, so visible, in Jesus' life that the disciples came to Him and asked, "Master, teach us to pray."

Jesus prayed often and was totally submissive to God the Father and He received or had tremendous inner strength and unlimited physical powers! I want to be like that!! I want to become totally submissive and my will totally dedicated to God–I want to be Christ like. I want to allow my inner spirit to be permanently and excitedly focused on God and the Holy Spirit!

Jesus drove moneychanger's (business people) out of the temple. Meaning?—It was not the easy, safe, comfortable thing to do but it was the "right" thing to do. Do we stand up for "God's ways" or do we take the comfortable route and keep quiet?

To be "Christ like" means to take a stand for God's ways and then live a life as an example for that belief.

We need to get close and personal with God. Why do people say "Praise <u>the</u> Lord"? Why not "Praise <u>My</u> Lord," or, "Praise You, My Lord." For you see my God wants a close and personal relationship!!

Oh Lord, help me to desire to do your will—make my enthusiasm and love for you a burning, raging fire that spreads quickly and grows larger and larger to those around me. Heavenly Father, help me to lean on you and trust you for all my needs. Don't let me ever forget:

This is my Father's World!!!!

P.S.

Be a "name dropper." When I was in the military I worked directly for our commander for awhile. Sometimes I would tell people to do things they did not want to take time to do. I might start my conversation with something like, "The commander wants this done this week." OR "The commander will be watching that everyone finishes this week." It often helps to put some real authority behind your message. I think Jesus and God and the Holy Spirit all know what is going on but we are taught to say things like, "in Jesus name we ask!" OR "I know that Jesus went to the cross for me and I am saved by grace!!"

Be a name dropper. I think that by speaking the name of Jesus we are strengthening our own faith and we will become bolder the more times we say the name of "Jesus." The Trinity likes us to give credit and praise and appreciation directed toward them lest we try to pat ourselves on the back and blaspheme the Holy Spirit.

I plan that when I stand before God—Jesus will come over and say, "This is my friend, James, and I have a mansion prepared for him."

Awhile back a bunch of the grandkids were visiting and I began to ask them for a ticket as they entered the house. When I got to Hannah she just matter-of-factly said, "I don't have to pay because you're my Grandpa!!!" Nobody could have said it better than that young child!! When I get to meet God I can say, "I don't have to pay—I'm your son and Jesus has already paid it all."

Disclaimer: Actually, I don't think I'll have to say anything— my Heavenly Father already knows my complete history and my relationship with Jesus before I get there.

Notes

Guilt and Forgiveness

CHAPTER 10

All my loved ones, I want you to have an understanding of guilt and forgiveness. I've known people who were "ate up" with guilt. That can be a terrible way to live and so needless because our God set up a way through which we can be forgiven and then move on through **grace**.

We are not of this world, but we must live in this world. Our world is heaven—living, walking, talking with God and everything is good and perfect. We must live in this world full of evil, lies, and doing wrong. Paul says Romans 7:18, 19, & 20 "...the evil I do not want to do–this I keep on doing." When we do wrong we need to ask forgiveness, make it right if possible, and then put it all behind us and accept and live in grace! Don't dwell on wrong doing of the past! Think of good things and God and Jesus.

Let's start back in Gen. 1:26-27 when God said, "Let us make man in our image..." That seems logical–since God was going to make a man, put him into a garden, and communicate with him for eternity it only makes sense to make man similar to himself. Man should even have the ability to live forever!! We don't all look physically alike and our bodies won't live forever, etc. so God must have made us like Himself as a spirit.

God created everything in the five days and said it was good. Then the sixth day He created man and said it was "<u>very</u> good." But when Adam and Eve sinned they surely felt ashamed and guilty. They knew they had done wrong—they realized they were naked. So they hid when God came around. They sewed leaves together to make coverings for themselves. God talked to them and explained their "punishment."

It is about the same with us. When we do something wrong we probably know it. Don't ignore or harden your heart. Secondly they felt guilty and ashamed and naked. They tried to "cover up" their feelings (made clothes). But our God sees and knows everything before we tell Him!

When someone comes by to talk to us about our "problem" we try to avoid them and their talk. Eventually we are cornered or we realize we need God's help. We need peace in our mind and heart again that can only come from giving everything over to God!

There has been a few times in my life that my sin seemed awfully heavy and I felt ashamed and lonely. In my mind, I imagine myself "going back to the cross." I think I walk back to the cross with Jesus on it and I kneel or lay at the foot of the cross. I cry and pray and I feel so overwhelmed by His presence. I think Jesus says something about taking all my sins away and that <u>He</u> will give me peace. His arms are wide open so that He can take them all!

Words cannot begin to tell you how I feel! It is as if Jesus knew I was coming. He is on the cross—the sin of the world of this world is on His Shoulders—God the Father will close His eyes to all the sin and Jesus feels rejected by the very people He came to love and lead—Yet I feel like Jesus (in all this stress and turmoil and pain and much more) knew I was coming and He cared about what was bothering me!!! This is the only way I can tell you how much Jesus loves ME and YOU!!! In the Spiritual realm of heaven there is no time. The cross covers all the past, present, and future all at once.

Today or some day or anytime you can stop where you are and ask forgiveness of sins. Sometimes I feel led to go to the church altar and get away from my "normal place in life". A few times in prayer I visualize that I take a "walk to the cross"—and I really, really encourage you to do this also. Kneel before the cross and—if you can—look up at Jesus and say "I'm sorry that I have sinned".

If, for whatever reason, we cannot turn our problems over to our God—then we will continue to live with this guilt and being ashamed!! We must get that sin and guilt out of our lives (given to God) or we will not find peace. Some people believe they have hurt or destroyed a part of God when they sin, but let me tell you a story.

I had some little kids draw pictures of me. They drew and colored until they had the best pictures they could do. I took the pictures and reminded the youngsters that they had made "images" of me. I took one picture and tore off an ear, and another an eye, and another the nose, and another picture I tore out the mouth. Then I asked the kids, "Did any of the things I did to the images destroy and hurt the original (me)?"

Now let me ask you, "Am I made in the spiritual <u>image</u> of God?? If I sin or do evil and wrong things will that destroy or hurt God's power or His omnipotence?" NO—nothing that I do will weaken or destroy a part of God. But don't sin or sadden God on purpose!!

I am ALSO made and live in the physical realm of this world. God is "above" the happenings of this world—He made this world! Yes, my wrong actions can start rumors and cause lots of problems—but not totally unrepairable. The Holy Spirit can change hearts and God can work through people as needed, but if you have any guilt it needs to end here and now. The pain needs to end—and God wants you to be forgiven, victorious, and free to worship, praise and witness for Him! God made us born pure and uncontaminated. He wants us back to that condition, or as close as possible, because He loves us.

Talk with God and ask Him to forgive you of ALL wrong. If you are angry at someone, etc., separate that person from their sin. Practice and learn to love that person while hating the sin they did.

VERY IMPORTANT: Separate the person from the sin action they did!! Learn to love the person but hate what they did. That way if they are/become a Christian this is what will happen:

1. You learn to love the person and hate their sin.
2. You both go to heaven.
3. The only thing you both take to heaven for eternity is your "love". So you will love each other forever.
4. No sin enters heaven—so their sin, or the memory of it, will not go with you but will be buried forever.
5. If someone wrongs you please separate the person from the actions and forgive them. Their wrong or sin is such a small part of eternity. If you have done something that causes you to live in the pain and shame of guilt—talk with God and ask forgiveness. God can and will forgive you of anything! Talk with God and get rid of the guilt and live to prepare yourself for a positive and happy eternity.

THEREFORE!! If you sin DON'T TRY TO COVER—UP and NEVER TRY TO IGNORE WHAT IS DONE!!!!!! GO TO GOD!!!! TALK TO GOD!!!!

I Thessalonians 5:16-18, "Be joyful always; pray continually; give thanks in all circumstances, for this is God's will for you in Christ Jesus." Live in constant prayer. If you live in constant communication with God, you are not likely to get into the life threatening situations with guilt. Living in guilt hurts but living in God's peace is wonderful!!

Let me explain what happens with us. All of us have sinned and fallen short of any prize. John 8:7, "...If any one of you is without sin let him be the first to throw a stone..." Then in Isaiah 53:6, "We all, like sheep, have gone astray, each of us has turned to his own way; and the Lord has laid on him (Jesus) the iniquity of us all." We were deep in sin and destined to Hell. Jesus came to this world, lived a perfect life, and willingly went to the cross with all the sins of the world on Him. By grace we are set free!! I can't understand all that was accomplished by Jesus going to the cross, but my sins were all taken away and God cannot remember them again!!!!

No matter what you have done–no matter what you have thought or said, no matter what age or sex or denomination you are–no matter anything—<u>JESUS HAS ALREADY PAID THE PENALTY FOR THE SINS YOU HAVE DONE OR WILL EVER DO!!!!!!!!!!!!!!!</u> THAT'S RIGHT JESUS PAID FOR YOUR SINS BEFORE YOU WERE EVEN BORN!!!! Already paid!!!!!!! All you have to do is accept Jesus as your Lord and Savior–Repent and ask him to forgive all your sins–He has already paid your dues. It's a gift to you and has already been paid and taken care of!!!

Jesus paid the price for us to get into heaven with all the options and accessories that go with the trip!!! NOW what do we do????? What will you do with this Jesus?????Now, thanks to Jesus, we are authorized to wear the big "G" on the front of our shirt:

The big "G" stands for the Gift of salvation as Jesus went to the cross to save us!! Jesus paid for ALL of our sins and ALL of our Guilt!!! Give up ALL Guilt & sin!!

You are under Grace—try to sin no more—but His Grace will cover you!! The Big" G stands for Grace!!"

Think about this a minute; no matter how "bad" you were Jesus will forgive you and His grace will cover you. Now, let's say that years later in life you make some bad choices and backslide awhile. Jesus forgave you before–don't you think He will forgive you again??? You can't be so "bad" that Jesus won't love and forgive you—He forgave you before—He wants to forgive you and have you as His child. Our God considers you a winner and in the last days Jesus will win the battle to prove:

This is my Fathers World!!!

We don't need to live in stress and guilt. Col. 2:13, "...God made you alive with Christ. He forgave us all our sins." Luke 6:37, "...Forgive and you will be forgiven."

Acts 10:43, "...everyone who believes in him (Jesus) receives forgiveness of sins through his name." Think about this a minute. When you believe in Jesus as the Son of God and live by His name, every sin and everything to do with sin is removed forever. If <u>all</u> sin is forgotten forever how could there be any guilt? Sin and guilt are to be gone!!

Please let me explain. One time—I'm not sure whether I was asleep or awake lying in bed. Something was bothering me—something that could develop into sin. Then I saw myself in an old prison like Saul/Paul was in. I was facing the wall and I felt that things were dark and hopeless and depressing and going towards a dead end, just like that wall. Then I turned around and I saw light and I felt God was there and I felt hope and alive—and the chains on my body fell to the floor and I began saying, "Thank you Jesus, Thank you God, I'm free, I'm free" and I left there feeling so weightless and alive and overjoyed!!

Philippians 3:13 says, "....forgetting those things that are behind and reaching forward to those things that are ahead." Give <u>everything</u> over to God. If there is one thing God cannot do–then He just as well do nothing. Believe me; it is so wonderful to be free! GOD WANTS YOU FREE, UNBLEMISHED IN ANY

WAY, UNHURT IN ANY WAY, TOTALLY FORGIVEN, OF PURE HEART, AND SOUL, AND MIND AND AS A LIVING SACRIFICE... Only by totally submitting ourselves to God's authority can we do that.

The first verses in Romans talks about being transformed by the renewing of your mind AND present your body acceptable to God.

In the Old Test, part of worship (acts of worship) was to bring a pure living offering to God, sometimes a lamb or a kid goat or a bird, etc. The sacrifice was to be pure–no physical defects or impurities!! These animals were then killed and sacrificed in various ways, as acts of worship, to cover all of their sin.

In the New Test, Jesus, who lived a perfect life without any sin, was tortured and beaten and then allowed himself to be killed on a cross!! He was the faultless and final sacrifice for all time. Now after Jesus did all that—as acts of worship we are to go before God as <u>living sacrifices</u> (Romans 12:1, "...offer your body as living sacrifices") We are to present our physical bodies and our spiritual being as pure and holy as possible covered by the blood of Jesus—ready to do God's will and work.

Ro. 12:2, "...be transformed by the renewing of your mind. Then you will be able to test and approve what God's will is" for you. So if you want to be closer to God you need to be transformed by the renewing of your mind. You will need to make a sincere effort to guide your mind and thoughts to praise and glorify your God. Align with Jesus as the perfect example and as your Friend.

God's work is as varied as there are workers! In other words; God does not need all preachers or all missionaries. He wants to carefully and selectively put together a team that will be ready for action 24 hours a day—7 days a week at every second and in every place and occupation where there are people.

For example: the Holy Spirit may wake you up in the middle of the night with the idea to pray for someone. A co-worker may ask you a question like "why are animals in the Christmas scene?" You are to sacrifice or give a small part of your life to God's will & work.

Jesus took care of our guilt and forgiveness 2,000 years ago when He went to the cross as a perfect sacrifice. He paid the price for all our sins. We are to just receive that gift of grace and forgiveness and then spread the word to other's that:

This is my Fathers World!!!

Don't just learn things that God has done or just stand and admire the beautiful rainbow and scenery that God makes—make a close relationship and get to know the God that made the rainbow! Learn that God loves us and cares about us. He created this world for us to live in. God planned everything down to the minor details. He made this world and then looked down upon it and said that it was good and everything was ready FOR US! Truly:

This is my Father's World!!!!

P.S. If you or someone you know is living in guilt or starting to feel depressed—Have them say the 23rd chapter of Psalms five or more times a day. Don't just say it—Think about each word and let it give you a sense of peace and security.

Notes

CROSSING THE RIVERS

CHAPTER 11

Crossing the Red Sea

One of the best known Bible stories is the story where Moses raises his hand and arm and God parts the Red Sea and the people walk through on a dry riverbed!! There are three things I want you to see in this story. First I want you to see that God did not take their problem away. He could have stopped the army of chariots at any time by different methods—but He knew that He had total power and the ultimate control over anything and everything that could happen so He allowed the chariots to keep coming for awhile. God wanted the Israelites to recognize that He took care of the incoming army without any problems.

Second, notice that God provided a safe and workable solution to their problem (Pharaoh's army was about to annihilate the entire Israel nation). He provided a safe and adequate route for the people to take. God may "help" you in different ways and different times. Notice that the people were upset and angry that God and Moses brought them out here to die. They did not talk of positive things, but rather they just gripe, grumble, and complain!

Third, notice that they had to walk through the riverbed of their miracle. As they walked on the dry riverbed I can imagine a very high wall of water right beside them. A wall of water splashing and raging around looking huge and powerful, and extremely scary every step of the way. They are reminded that the only way to survive this huge and scary ordeal is by the power and loving care of a great God. They may remember all the grumbling and complaining they had been doing and how they were mad at God. Now they realize how powerful God is and their relationship of total weakness and how small they are compared to this God!!

Remember, we are supposed to be developing a personal relationship with our savior and creator. We need to develop a relationship of love, understanding, and trust. Look at that first sentence in the first paragraph "One of the best -----." I often hear that Moses raised his arm and parted the Red Sea. That is not very wrong—but it is certainly not right! I want you to understand why. God parted the Red Sea WHEN MOSES DID WHAT HE WAS TOLD TO DO!!!!!! God could have told Moses to stand in the middle of the river, or touch his staff to the river water, or anything else. God could have told the priests to stand in the middle of the river—that would have looked real "religious." But instead He told Moses to hold up his arm. It is not up to us to choose the way to get things done–it is up to us to get done what we are told to do!

So imagine this now!? Moses is standing on a small mount overlooking the river and a couple of people seem to be standing with him. Moses has his arm extended out. The people seem very rushed as they try to hurry the animals and kids across the river bed. The sheep want to run the other way—maybe afraid of the high wall of water. The camels don't want to hurry—they can see no danger so why waste the energy. The kids are fascinated by the wall of water and want to put their hands into it but are afraid so just stand and dare each other while their Mom's are running crazy trying to find their own children. What a situation and the parents know that–although they are getting across the river the army will soon be upon them because God did not take that huge <u>problem</u> away and they may all die.

Romans 12:2 "Do not conform any longer to the pattern of this world, but be transformed by the renewing of your mind. Then you will be able to test and approve what God's will is– His good, pleasing, and perfect will." So God had told Moses to stand there and raise his arm and then He would work a miracle. Probably more general, this verse says that if I/we want to get into a condition that God can use us–we must not conform to this world and we must have our minds renewed or retuned to our God and creator's ways.

Crossing the Jordan

My favorite Bible story is Joshua 3:14–4:9 when Joshua led the Israelites into the Promised Land. It was a miracle when God held back the waters of the Jordan River and the people walked across the dry riverbed!!!

Wonderful story–a rare story–where everything is going perfectly. The priests are to carry the ark through the river–they step into the river–and as they step down, the water backs up and their foot comes down on dry ground! Perfect... The people saw their miracle begin to happen when the first two priests carrying the ark stepped into the "water"!! They had the faith that something great was about to happen and they were "on the move." All the people follow. Perfect... (I wonder how many things we miss because we don't just step out in faith and "go".)

The Israelites are walking with God's care and help. (If they were walking in God's will they would have been in the Promised Land years ago.) They are not pushed; they are not threatened right now like their ancestors had been when the Pharaoh of Egypt was chasing after them. They are nervous because there may be giants in the new land and there may be hard wars and battles to fight but are of their own free will moving forward and following what they believe is God's plan for them and they are expecting miracles and many answers to prayers!

As they move forward a representative from each of the 12 tribes will take a stone from the middle of the river bottom: These 12 stones—out of the middle of their Miracle—are used to build a monument=Out of the middle of their miracle they built a monument with these 12 stones in a field near the river so they will never forget the miracles God did as He led them into the Promised Land.

Later in life as they walk past this monument they are to remember and talk about this miraculous day. One they are Never to forget. Story telling from generation to generation was the way that information was kept alive in their people and how events were passed on through the generations.

I often tell parents—take pictures, start scrapbooks, start a memory shelf or a memory box or something for your child's Christian life. Example: when I was a child through teenager our Sunday school gave attendance pens. I have a long row of attendance pens that I am authorized to wear!! I am proud of these lapel pens and I keep them in a box. They remind me of many events that happened while I was growing up. These pens, my baptism certificate, and a silly cap I wore at a men's retreat, and many more things remind me of my "growing up" in my spiritual life. At our church the kids in the youth groups get a "T" shirt or cap or something as they progress. You don't need to keep these items forever–take pictures and keep a book. I know at least one family that celebrates the yearly anniversary of their child's baptism. WOW! That is so terrific.

Several times the Israelites did not believe and trust God to take care of them and protect them. If I really want to share in the promises and protection of God I have to start accepting his word and his protection and MOVE FORWARD!! The doubters and disbelievers usually don't get anywhere!!! OH Lord, help me to believe, trust, and move out in FAITH where you want me to go!

Let me stop a minute and look back through history. In the beginning God created the heavens and earth and it was <u>good</u> (Gen 1:21). God created a man and a woman and put them in the Garden of Eden and all was <u>very good.</u> (Gen 1:31) This was the perfect will of God—He and the people would be "close" enough to walk and talk in the cool of the day!!! That He would be our Father and we would be His beloved children. But as time went by they sinned and were removed from God's perfect plan.

Later God prepared the Promised Land for His people—but they doubted Him and sinned against Him. As God tried to lead them to this Promised Land they accused God of just taking them out of Egypt to die in the desert. God lead the people through the Red Sea to escape being killed by the Pharoses' army. God tried to take care of His people by this acceptable plan but the people were not accepting. (When God leads you somewhere He has a plan and it will be <u>very good</u>!!)

<u>God promised</u> the Israelites they would have a land of milk and honey. Moses sent the 10 spies in to check it out. They came back: 8 say negative things and 2 say positive things. The people rebel because they believe and accept the negative 8 people. God killed the 8 and the Israelites are sent to live in the hard and tough desert until they die and never get to see the Promised Land? Why? Because they failed to put their total trust in God.

That brings us up to this day in history—the day that God leads His people across the Jordan River!! At last; the acceptable will of God. God has created previous perfect plans and then acceptable plans and ways for the people to live in harmony with Him. But the people rejected those plans of harmony and peace and live with fear and confusion (as at the Red Sea) and fear of the unknown future (as the big giants they will have to fight in the Promised Land).

Finally GOD ACCEPTS the people, just the way they are–rebellious sinners, who easily loose or give up their faith in Him when things start to look like trouble. Here we see that despite the way the people have been–God gave them a grand and beautiful entrance into the Promised Land. It was a place He had prepared for them when they cried out from Egypt. It was an answer to their prayers and beyond any doubt I believe it was much greater and much better than they could have imagined!! It wasn't totally free. They had to take an active part–they had to move in faith that God would be with them and that they would be God's people. They had to move across the land and "clean house!"

If we believe and step out in faith, we will enter a "promised Land" of closeness with Him. God still prepares great and wonderful miracles and/or places for His people today!! Do we quickly and eagerly follow God wherever He tries to take us?? Do we accept the many blessings and gifts that He wants to GIVE us? REMEMBER THIS——God will ACCEPT you wherever you are and whenever you are ready and whatever your past. He will give you a peace and a purpose. He will accept you; no matter what your past, just like He accepted the Israelites and gave them a grand and spectacular entrance into the beautiful land of milk and honey. He wants to lead you and He wants to lead me. Praise God that He does not give up!!

God has prepared or is preparing good things for us in this life! When the Israelites crossed the river the first priests caring the ark had to step out as if they were stepping into water but having the great faith that their foot would go down onto a dry riverbed. They had to have great faith. There may be great times of "milk and honey" in front of us BUT we have to walk up to the river and put our foot in–take that huge step in total faith that the river bed will be completely dry so that we do not slide and fall in the mud!!!

This time God parted the river for them as a grand entry into the land He had promised them, a grand entry after waiting and wandering through the desert 40 years, a grand entry into a land that finally would be theirs, a land of milk and honey and all the good things in life. A land that would be theirs and then their children's and then their grandchildren, Etc...

I like the part where a representative from each of the tribes picked up a stone from the center of the river (from the center of their miracle) and together they made an altar to worship God and thank Him for bringing them to this land. The memorial will be there for years and years to remind them of the trip! I challenge each of you reading this book–each of you trying to walk a life with Jesus–each of you get a notebook and every time you see God helping you in some way–and each time you are in a miracle from God or someone else gets a miracle–write it in your notebook or when prayers are answered–write it down. Or when you get or are in a miracle or God helps provide special things for you or answers to prayers write them down. Keep the notebook as a reminder, each time you see it, that God is helping you.

God parted the River Jordan; the people walked into the Promised Land on the dry riverbed and then built an altar to praise God for bringing them there. This was a magnificent entry—because God loved the people and wanted the best for them.

God parted the Red Sea and the Israelites escaped from being destroyed by the Egyptian army. But with Joshua the river was parted so the people could go into the Promised Land. There was no real hurry or immediate need for them to get to the other side— there was nobody chasing them! There was no harm coming that they should need to hurry!

Our God can lead us through the obstacles in life just like He helped the Israelites through these two rivers that were in their way.

This is My Father's World!!!!

P.S. Stand out and make a spectacle of yourself=walk around Jericho every day with the people laughing at you.

NOTE: When I think about the Israelites and how God led them in these two stories the song "He didn't bring us this far to leave us" comes to my mind. I think of this song a lot.

However the song assumes that we are following God wherever **He** wants us to go! It assumes that we are NOT being led by SELF. If God brought us to certain level or place then He will take care of us. We want to live in His plan, His protection, His guidance, His care, His love, and His grace. For truly:

This is my Father's World!!!!

Notes

Good Enough

CHAPTER 12

Let's look at these Israelites wandering through the desert for 40 years. In some ways life has been really subdued and boring, day after day the same old scenery–sand, sand, and sand–once in a while a few blades of grass. It may not be that bad, but it seems like it to me. If you have been through one sand storm you have been through a hundred sand storms! Usually the good menu is the same old thing–quail and bread. What they would give for a big juicy filet steak or ribs cooked so good they are falling off the bone, and can be cut with a fork.

No matter how good things are going, sooner or later, people start wishing for something better or different. At the same time we resist any changes and argue to do things the same way we have always done them. We feel more secure and safe in our "known" world and resist the "unknown."

Imagine now as the Israelites are getting closer to the Jordan River and the entrance into the Promised Land. This will be a land of milk and honey–it will be the opposite of this desert trip. They will be able to live in a HOUSE and not have to take the tent down in the morning and carefully fold it up just right so it will fit in that little bag! We did our share of living in a tent while our kids were growing up. We have a lot of wonderful memories–but we did not have to live in it and move around for years and years and then some more years.

The thoughts of "going into the land of unknowns" creeps into the Israelites conversations and some of the people are not sure if they are excited to enter the land or not. They "know what they have now" and the uncertainty of the future can be very exciting but very scary at the same time.

In these times of uncertainty some of the 12 tribes looked around and said, "It looks pretty good right here." I imagine this as an area right along the edge of the desert with water and some green grass. It's not all bad and not all good. "We could build our homes here and grow vineyards and wheat and corn and make pastures for our animals: we'll have a good life right here." The tribes of Reuben, Gad, and the half tribe of Manasseh wanted to stay just outside the Promised Land, so God granted their desires. But first, they had to go into the Promised Land and help fight the wars to conquer and secure the land as originally intended. Then they could go back to this area and live.

Unfortunately, these people settled for the "OK life" that they could see instead of going into the unknown that God had prepared for them. They accepted the average/ok life when they could have gone just a little bit further and received the beautiful and prosperous life style God had prepared for them. Their desire, dedication, and total devotion to God's plan stopped just short of reaching the Promised Land. That is sad because they had wandered through the wilderness for 40 years with so much heartache, death, and unknown. They got almost to the really great place God has prepared and they stopped and felt that this place was good enough.

I wonder why they were willing to settle down and live BEFORE they got to the land of milk and honey that God had promised. Were they afraid of the foreign people and did not want to go to battle with them? Maybe they thought there would not be enough land to go around and they could have more land here. Maybe they were tired of the Jewish leaders and wanted to be on their own—or—my favorite-when they looked around at the land they were standing on, they thought, "This is good enough land and we can raise crops here and have enough cattle. Let's just stay right here. Here we know and see what we have. If and when we go into the Promised Land it may not be as good as this." In other words—for whatever reason—They stopped before they got to the place God was preparing for them and I'm sure they settled for less.

I'm sure we do that too. I sometimes stopped before I got to the beautiful place God was preparing and I settled for second best when God was trying to lead me a little bit farther. People are usually most comfortable where they are, or where they have been. God may have a better place for us to be: or a higher spiritual walk with Him but we may be reluctant because it may require more time or money or doing things we don't "feel comfortable doing."

Guess what?? I think that is often true! When I get to walking and talking with our God I find that I often get past my comfort zone! It is not as bad as I thought it would be because God is there to help me and give me a feeling of peace. Probably the thing I did not want to do was visitation. Now I usually leave the person with the feeling—that was rather enjoyable, I'm glad I went.

Sometimes I think I have a good enough understanding or relationship with my God. I may have said to myself, "I'm not required or expected to spend too much of my time with the Lord's work, and I need time to do the things I have to do in life." I may be just like the Israelites that stopped just short of the beautiful and plentiful place in my Christian walk that God has prepared for me. But now I feel ready to proceed further in my Christian walk. It's kind of like climbing steps. When I feel ready and reach a point in my Christian life God raises me up and I do something and learn something and then He'll raise me up a little more. I'm not high enough to see everything yet but I'm gaining slowly—one step at a time.

Along this same line—one of my favorite verses is James 4:8. "Come near to God and he will come near to you. Wash your hands, you sinners, and purify your hearts, you double-minded."

When I was a teenager I spent a lot of my summers working for my Grandpa Temple on his wheat and cattle farm near Hays, Kansas. We didn't have cabs on the tractors or combines and that part of Kansas is dry with lots of dust, so when I came in from the field I'd be really dirty. When I went to the house to eat there was a water faucet that we sometimes watered tomatoes with in the front yard and Grandpa had a little table there with a wash pan and soap. I would wash up before going to the house. I had a short flat top hair cut and I'd take my hat off and wash my whole head and wash my arms up to my elbows. Washing up was exciting–because I knew something wonderful was about to happen!! I'd be dreaming of that wonderful fried chicken! I'd wash fast, as I smelled the delicious aroma, so I could hurry to the kitchen table and eat!

Now, I'll tell you the truth–My Grandma made the best fried chicken, mashed potatoes, and chicken gravy in the world! (Going through high school I don't think anyone could eat more than I did. **I am an authority on good food**!!) I have eaten chicken for many years and in several countries and I'd give my Grandma top award.

I read that verse in James 4:8 and my mind flashed back to me washing up in a hurry to get ready for Grandma's fried chicken. That chicken was like a reward for working there. And my mind said, "Wash your hands, you sinners…" If I will wash my hands and arms and head and heart and mind and soul, I believe God is preparing something wonderful for me. I'm excited!!

When I was a kid I'd open the door to the house and I'd smell that dinner cooking and there was no where I'd rather be. Now, I'm excited because I know my God is preparing something for me–I need to get cleaned up so that I can open that door and receive the blessings that God is preparing for me!!!!

Are you excited yet??? Do you know that God is preparing great things for you if you don't settle for something less????

This verse (James 4:8) started with "Come near to God and he will come near to you." First we are to seek God, to search the Bible to get to know him, to be led by the Spirit so that every thought is striving to live following Him. This also says you may be saved and you may know God, but you may be walking through life at a distance from God and dragging one foot slowly in the "world!" Talk with God all day long; meditate on his word, the Bible, everywhere you go. Try to live close to God in all we say and do and He will come near and hold us. Not just that He will come close to me, but, that He will hold me and love me and I will feel comfortable that:

This is my Father's World!!!!

P.S. Get to know God and recognize the things He does for you! As you get to know Him, open your heart, your mind, your finances, your time, and your habits then, your way of life will change and God will come in and become the leader of your life.

Statistics

When you see statistics, I want you to think and reason before you decide if they mean anything.

Statistics can be found on most any subject. There is an old saying that goes something like "figures never lie and liars always figure". I sometimes get a laugh out of the way we people figure statistics. One survey showed that 90 % of United States citizens say they pray. Now, that leads me to believe 90 of 100 people talk to God or a supreme being. My question is what value does knowing the percentage of people that say they pray really have for us? VERY LITTLE! To start with, I guess, I don't believe the statistic is true—I don't believe 90% of us pray! AND, just the fact that a person talks to God does not mean they are going to heaven or anything. I could visit and talk to Bill Gates all day but that does not make me an heir to the good life!

Jesus said that not everyone that cries Lord, Lord will enter the Kingdom of Heaven. I agree there are a lot of people that mention God's name during the day but not with the same meaning you and I would.

My guess (out of the clear blue) is that maybe 90% of Americans have talked to themselves. Well, tell me seriously—have you talked to yourself?? What value is my statistic? NONE!

Someday you may want to look at some statistics about church growth or attendance, belief's people have, evangelistic figures, or whatever. I am saying you need to be very careful when looking at statistics. Be sure they are done with a completely open mind.

My favorite scientific story goes like this: A young zealous scientist was doing some research to support his statistics. He got his white smock, a clipboard, a freshly sharpened pencil, a tape measure and a frog. For the base measurement, he put the frog on the floor at a starting line and said, "Jump frog jump". The frog jumped, and the excited young man took out his tape measure and measured the jump and then wrote on his clipboard "five feet". He then cut off one of the frog's legs. He put the frog on the starting line and again said, "Jump frog jump." Again he took out his tape measure and measured the jump. The frog had jumped four feet. He cut off the second leg and put the frog on the starting line and said "Jump frog jump." The frog jumped and this time the measurement was three feet. He cut off the third leg, carefully set the frog at the starting line and said, "Jump frog jump." He wrote on the clipboard, two foot. Now the scientist was really excited that he was seeing such consistent results. He cut off the last leg, set the frog on the starting line and said, "Jump frog jump." The frog didn't move! The young man picked up his clipboard and filled out the "summary section" with the following statement: "Obviously, when the legs were removed from the frog it could no longer hear!" What looks so obvious may not be true at all.

When teaching in High School I had students that wanted to talk a lot. They wanted to tell me everything they knew— the problem is people rarely learn while they are talking. In the military I went through some outstanding truck mechanic courses and was often at the top of my class. Why, because I love mechanics and wanted to be good at it AND spent a lot of time studying the books and listening to gain more knowledge. I became a top rated truck mechanic because I listened to seek out knowledge and search for truth and facts to help me acquire the skills needed. The reward was a very successful career.

Our spiritual life works the same way! If we talk constantly to God we may not progress as quickly as we desire. We need to spend some time studying the Bible and quietly listening for God to guide us and give us understanding in some way. We need to seek out knowledge and search for truth and facts to help us in our Christian walk.

We live in a busy fast paced world. We can take a little time to talk to God as we ride a bus, car, or train to work each day. But, if we want to prepare for a successful future, we need to actually take some time to go after and seek first His Kingdom and His Righteousness–Matthew 6:33. This requires listening and Bible study and not just talking to God.

Deuteronomy 30:19-20 "...that you may love the Lord your God, listen to His voice and hold fast to Him...." John 10:27 "My sheep listen to my voice; I know them and they follow me." Proverbs 1:5 "let the wise listen and add to their learning..." James 1:22 "Do not merely listen to the word and so deceive yourselves–Do what it says!" Read James 1:23-25 also!

So, if you are to live a Christian life:

1. Pray often.
2. Listen to seek knowledge about God, Jesus, and the Holy Spirit.
3. Search the word of God and actively live by faith.
4. DO IT!! James 1:22

Therefore, what does a survey asking, "Do you pray", really determine? Maybe it shows that some people believe there is a God of some kind. That question has to be followed by another question, "If you believe there is a God to pray to—What do you do with that information???" Knowledge that God exists rarely has any value until you decide to live a life of faith and believe that:

This is My Father's World!!!

Note

The Christmas Story

CHAPTER 13

It is Christmas 2008 and we are celebrating the birth of our savior. The world was not expecting the savior of the Jews to be born in an animal hay feeder, nor was he expected to arrive at this busy time of year. The world was not prepared to have a welcome party for Jesus under these circumstances. Let's take a look.

How would you feel if the president of the United States made a law–all of us had to go back to where we were born or a town that our relatives would call our home in order to pay taxes and have a census taken? My Dad and his brothers spread out from near Hays, Kansas.

So now visualize all my cousins and all our families meeting at a hotel in Hays a few days and paying the taxes. We'd spend a lot of time visiting and laughing and joking and glad to see each other. We'd have a really good time (without alcohol)—although you can imagine some of the taxpaying families would.

Just imagine now that a man and his very, very pregnant wife came into town. They have traveled a long way but the "NO VACANCY" sign is lit up on all the hotels so they stay in a hay barn on the edge of town and in the night their baby is born. This was "THE EVENT" of all history throughout all the universes!!!! There had to be rejoicing!! (I'm reminded of another story in Luke 19:38-40 when Jesus said that if the crowd of people did not cry out and identify Him "… the stones will cry out.")

The angels may have looked around town and seen families that had partied too much, many people were too tired from traveling, some parents just want to get their kids to bed, some parents carried their sleepy kids in to bed and tried not to wake them (memories of when I was younger) and some families that were having so much fun they would not want to be interrupted just because a baby is born, after all, the man to free the world and save all the Jews would not be born like this!!

Then may be the angels noticed a group of people that work 365 days a year. The shepherds are with their sheep everyday making sure they have grass to eat, water to drink, and are safe from predators. Many days they are moving on so there will be grass for the sheep to eat. Since they're always watching and moving they don't have shelter or corrals for the sheep at night. The shepherds take turns at night protecting the sheep from coyotes and other wild animals. (Can you see why Jesus is known as the good Shepherd?)

I visualize that the sheep and the shepherds were relaxed that night and maybe there was a full moon of good light. The angels may have thought, "The shepherds are not too busy to go visit the baby." I think to be a good Shepherd a person needs to be peaceful and gentle with lots of patience. They probably get pleasure from the smallest joys in life and especially a little baby.

A good shepherd probably loves life and all kinds of animals. He/she may take time to enjoy the wild flowers and the beauty that most people walk right over. Shepherds were a good choice— so the angels told them that a Savior was born and lying in a manger!! The shepherd's may have picked someone to stay with the sheep and the rest (Luke 2:16) hurried off to find the baby and praise him.

The Shepherd's were excited and that excitement continued as they told their story day after day as they traveled to find grass for their sheep. (They may have been the first missionary evangelists as they continuously told the story of how the angels had visited them and how they got to see the baby Jesus!!!)

Now, I want to back up and look at two main characters, Joseph and Mary. The angel had came and told Mary what was to happen in Luke 1:38. Mary answered "I am the Lord's servant…, May it be to me as you have said."

Mary knew that she could not be pregnant and that this story was not possible—BUT—she knew God!!! In Luke 1:37 the angel says, "For nothing is impossible with God." Mary believed that more than anything in this world. She was like an optimist who says, "It's impossible for us but God can do it. We need to pray and then start getting ready for the baby."

Gma Susan is an optimist! Sometimes she says things like, "The Bible said, God will, so let's go. Just pray and give it all to Jesus." (Don't tell anyone I said this—but sometimes it just doesn't seem that easy! Example, there may be repercussions coming that I may be nervous about.) Susan is right–why should I fear the unknown coming if I stand beside God?

Let's look at Joseph. Go to Matt. 1:18-21. The angel Gabriel has already visited Mary (Luke 1:26-39) and I'm sure Mary has explained everything she knows to Joseph. Now Joseph has to make decisions. Does he believe this happened to Mary or was it all just a dream? Should he separate from her? Should he continue toward their marriage? Who really made her pregnant? Questions go on and on. (The first problem is that Joseph is a man. Nowhere in Matt. 1:18-20 does it say that Joseph stopped to ask directions!!) Verse 19 says Joseph is a righteous man and he seems to care deeply about Mary's feelings and what people will think. He thinks of several things to do and goes right to "divorce her quietly" (Matt. 1:19).

Stop here a minute: Matthew 1:19 says Joseph is a righteous man. The righteous shall live by their faith—the unrighteous shall live by their own desires (Habakkuk 2:4). Therefore, Joseph must have been a man of great faith. Luke 1:28 says the angel said to Mary, "… you who are highly favored! The Lord is with you." Later Gabriel said, "Mary, you have found favor with God." Here are two people that GOD HAS CHOSEN FOR THE GREATEST EVENT IN HISTORY!!!!!!!!!!!!!! They should be in perfect harmony but that is not always the case. After hearing Gabriel's speech Mary probably told Joseph everything. He should have been excited but instead he began thinking of ways to quietly get rid of her! Do things like this happen in our churches, our families, and our friendships?? Why? You may be near the best prayer partner possible but incompatible feelings could ruin things.

The second thing I notice is that it is mostly Mary's story. Joseph may feel left out because this is "all and only" about Mary. Mary has found favor with God—Mary will have a baby (and there may be a doubt of the father.) Mary will raise the Messiah, the Savior of the world.

Then in Matt. 1:20 the angel came to Joseph—now he gets first hand information right from an angel!!! Now he is involved! All of this became REAL and POSSIBLE and FACT as he saw and heard and believed that God was at work in all this. Joseph was a common carpenter with a simple life. All the happenings are going so fast–and to be Jesus' Dad–that's almost too much too fast!!

Joseph was surely overwhelmed with everything happening. (Sometimes everything happens all at once!!) It was really serious trouble when an unmarried girl became pregnant!! Society can be very cruel! And then the government ads this trip to go pay taxes and Joseph has to prepare for this trip soon. Don't forget the wood shop–Joseph probably had several things he was supposed to get finished for the customers and it is difficult to work late at night with only candles. (Between working in town, farming, and working in the shop–I usually don't volunteer very quickly for other things. However, I try to do what I'm really sure God wants me to do. I am just barely learning.)

It is OK to question things about God as long as you are prepared to accept any answer. You may or may not get an answer you expect or like. I often think of doubting Thomas (John 20:26-29). People talk and I'm sure everyone in the room knew of Thomas and his doubts. Jesus did not ridicule Thomas or call him an unbeliever or get mad at him. I think Jesus saw doubting Thomas as a witness in the future and it strengthened everyone's personal witness as Thomas verified it all! Because they watched Thomas, the people in that room will STAND BOLD and never waver in their faith!!

I realize that I have some of "doubting Thomas" in me too. Jesus gave Thomas the privilege or opportunity to touch the wounds and feel for himself: not as a hand me down story, but for himself. The story is FACT and Thomas actually touched the wounds himself so that he could tell others what he actually touched. I'm thinking particularly of when the Holy Spirit woke me up and said "Pray for someone." I can tell that story as a witness to others—I can tell that story to strengthen and excite me when I'm "down"—I can tell that story as fact and believable because it was ME.

So again I urge all of you; "Keep a notebook of your spiritual life and things that happen to you. This will someday encourage and strengthen you and can make you a great witness to others."

I'll tell you a recent quick story. Susan and I had to go to Wichita a while back. We drove into a restaurant for breakfast but it was not open yet so we went down the street to another restaurant. A young waitress limped to our table, took our order and said she had pulled several ligaments in her ankle. A little later a flash bulletin went across my mind, "Pray for her ankle." I'm sure I heard it right but I'm not an outgoing brave person. My first thought is total fear!!! I've never been so bold as to pray for a waitress AND WORSE YET—there are tables of people around us!! Maybe she won't come back to our table! Second thought—I often run things past Susan (I don't understand how some people live without a Bible believing, sincerely praying spouse). She just said, "OK."

The waitress did come back. "Could we pray for your ankle?" We three held hands and I prayed. She went on to work and we left. I don't know anymore about her. I prayed for her a few days and then she left my mind. But, I feel the biggest part of that was a test or training for me! If I'm sure God wants me to do something I need to "Just do it!" When God gives an assignment He provides the strength and a way. Often times I'll do something I think is for someone else and then realize that even more so it was for me to learn something. Lately I sense that I am to "be bold" and pray for people regardless of how I feel about the environment. (Jesus was a rebel, always bold and outspoken. He often upset even the church leaders—He definitely was not shy.) This was a God controlled event to build my confidence and boldness around people.

I'm going to tell you a couple stories as well as I can. I asked Jesus into my life at a young age and I believed that Jesus, the Son of God, died on the cross for me and rose again and is preparing a place for me in heaven. I was baptized in Cedar Bluff Lake in Kansas as a teenager.

In my 40's I began to seriously see that God wants to be close to me and to help me in my life, right here and now—not just to go to heaven. As I went through my 50's I could see more and more times that God helps others, and me, through situations.

As I neared my 60's every day I prayed that I wanted to be closer to God. I wanted to know His voice. I'm glad that someday I'm going to heaven—BUT for many more years I'm going to need help getting through this world. James 4:8 "Come near to God and he will come near to you." I believe the God that created the universe and everything in it is in me!! This King of all kings and Lord of lords and Creator of all things is in me!! This God that owns the cattle on a thousand hills is in me and cares about me!! Cares enough that Jesus went to the cross!!

My biggest enemy is myself. I pray that each of you will walk closer to God than I, and know beyond any doubt you will be blessed!!

I began to see that God really wants to tell us things as we become more mature in our spiritual lives. Many things are too complicated or too advanced for our minds—so God desires to communicate according to our desire and abilities.

I want to try to tell you exactly how to talk with God but it is beyond my words. Most important I think is to know and praise God as the creator of the universe and all that is in it! God is the ultimate power. Then thank God that Jesus went to the cross as the ultimate love. Be aware of our position according to God's position. Ask that all sin and barriers between you and God be forgiven. Explain what you need or need to know. As you pray KNOW that God has the power to do anything or nothing—I think it is important that you pray and ask, communicate with God—BUT you have to be preparing and willing to accept any answer! End your prayer with something like, "Thy will be done," and mean it!! There may be many answers to your prayer questions. If you cannot live with ANY one of the answers I think you are not totally praying effectively. End with "thy will be done" and KNOW that ultimately you will accept whatever God chooses to do.

Like I said before, the most important thing is our relationship with God. **Is** the God you worship Sunday morning the same God you pray to and listen to and worship while you go through Thursday, and all the week??

I desire to walk closer and closer to my God and Savior. I'm going to spend forever and ever with God and I know my life on earth is better because of God's help–as much as I let Him help.

I might sometimes say God answers prayers that are in His direct will. But that statement is too limited. God has answered prayers just because I asked AND I have had prayers that are answered "NO" or don't seem to be answered at all, or I forget. I wish I could explain better or write out exact prayers you could use word for word. However, I encourage you to simply "pray from your heart" be open and be honest. Don't be concerned about sentences or design. The Lord's Prayer is an "example" to help teach us. If we sing "What a friend we have in Jesus", how would we talk to Him? Walk close to God so that you can talk, share ideas and listen too.

We should seek answers, knowledge and wisdom directly from God. James 3:17-18 says, "...the wisdom that comes from heaven is first of all pure; then peace loving, considerate, submissive, full of mercy and good fruit, impartial and sincere. Peacemakers who sow in peace raise a harvest of righteousness." ((((I have had some instant healing where God took the pain and cause away. I sometimes hear things like, "God doesn't do things like that anymore." First, if my God has the desire and the power to forgive all my sins–physical healing would be no trouble. Second, is this or is this not the same God that is in the Bible? Therefore, the question is not "can God" but rather "will God" perform miracles as I ask. There are a lot of times I don't know WHY things happen the way they do—but I know that too often if there is a problem it is me. I have to be a NEW person and free from sin. That famous ole donkey of Balaam's had absolutely no talent, but that donkey also had absolutely no sin in it. I have to get as good as that donkey!! God will provide and teach me the talent part but I have to get on my knees and allow God to help me with the sin part.)))

Now let's look back at Joseph—after the angel explained things to Joseph he became part of the program. He took Mary home as his wife. He took care of Mary and named the baby, Jesus.

I put this Christmas story in for several reasons. First, I want you to understand that this story just came to my mind and I wrote it this year. Every year I see the basic story as it is written about the birth of Jesus. I am also seeing a new side story each year.

THE BIBLE IS LIKE NO OTHER BOOK!!!!!!! Sometimes I read the same words and I get a different story!!!! Study the Bible and it will become exciting. The Living Word has different meanings and characteristics to each of us according to what we need at this time in our lives.

Are we ready to go? If the angels had told us Jesus was born would we go honor Him?? Are we getting ready and are we prepared if an angel came to us and said God has selected you for a mission—will you decide to accept it?

Then is our relationship with God strong enough to get us through our assignments? Always remember, we know the end of the story about what happens on this earth and we know that:

This is my Father's World!!!!

Notes

Meet with Believers

CHAPTER 14

In this chapter you are the pilot, so get into your flight suit and prepare for takeoff. Your ETD (estimated time of departure) is NOW. Your point of contact will be the highest Universe Commander Father God. You'll get your briefings during Sunday school and Church and then be sent out into the world on a mission!! You have a job to do.... You may feel that you are alone— but you never will be alone. Our church has a very active prayer chain if you run into danger. Our church has a very good support team that meet to "refuel" you on Sunday mornings and a prayer support team that meets on Tuesday for any special maintenance concerns you may encounter in life!!

This world was never meant to be a one person military operation against the enemy. You were meant to be part of a team. Remember in Genesis when God created the earth and then He made Adam. Right after that they were all looking for a help mate for Adam. So you see, even in the beginning Adam was not supposed to live life alone!! God got him a helpmate.

You are a pilot and you have a mission—if you decide to accept it!!! It's not an easy mission and there will be struggles and temptations, but you are required to try to maintain a consistent and never wavering positive faith pattern. God will provide you with the latest and greatest protective equipment that will ensure and guarantee a successful, "Mission accomplished!!" A list of your protective offensive/defensive equipment is discussed in Ephesians 6: 11-18. The last item is the sword which is both a defensive and offensive weapon system. The sword is only valuable if you practice, practice, and more practice–read the training manual (Bible) consistently! That training manual contains 66 books and should include defensive information for any enemy you could encounter. There is some overlap and good continuity between the individual books. God will be with you 24/7 and will never leave or disavow you. The ending is already known and guaranteed–YOU WILL WIN!!

I don't have very positive feelings about our world as we get toward the end of times. I fear the church buildings will become more of a social gathering place than a place where true devotional Christians gather. I hope you all keep meeting with true Bible based Christians wherever they meet. I wonder if a few churches make their rules and beliefs according to society's standards and expectations rather than according to God's rules.

In Luke 9:49 the disciples came to Jesus and said that a man was casting out demons in His name so they tried to stop him. Jesus said not to stop him that there may be other people preaching Jesus to the crowds.

It's a tough decision to pick the "right" group to worship with. Don't feel rushed to decide.

There are many reasons you should meet with the church (the church here is God's family of people). Romans 12:13 says, "... share with God's people who are in need." That could be mentally and spiritually as well as financially. I have been blessed in a lot of ways. I have been in the church position where I got to take money from unidentified givers to people in the church family that needed it. What an honor! If I could judge by feelings—it's not about money—you can sense the Holy Spirit working and the love of the fellowship in these times! It's about doing what you feel God wants you to do!

Here's our story. My job in the military kept me overseas 15 years whether I wanted to or not!! We often talk about holidays where we would invite a few or half dozen or so single military to our home to celebrate. When we were young and had some little kids to buy Christmas presents, food, and fun things for–it took all we were paid. We would often receive some unexpected financial help from anonymous people in our church.

Now you need to understand–when I was growing up we were quite independent. I'd bet my Dad broke down farm machinery flat tires with large screwdrivers, patched the tire, and reassembled them by himself until he was 70 years old. I was not that self-sufficient or that tough!! I was independent and people giving me something did not go very well with me! Then, somehow my God had a training moment with me, an individual that gave me money did it because he/she felt that God wanted them to do it. It did not matter if they even wanted to do it, or if they felt they could afford it. All that really mattered in the very end is that they were doing what they believed God wanted them to do! God will bless them for their obedience! Now, if I refuse to accept it I will ruin their joy of obedience and I'd be telling God I don't want to live by His ways! So if I believe that my God has the right plan for my life then I need to learn to follow His ways. That was a really big eye opener for me.

In later years, we gave money directly, or indirectly, through our church to help people. Like I said it is not about the money or the time we sometimes take to help someone or perhaps taking food to a shut in—it's the joy we get from following our God's directives and feeling as part of the family.

Heb. 10:24-25 talks about encouraging one another and to spur one another toward love and good deeds. I Peter 3:8 says,

"...live in harmony with one another; be sympathetic, love as brothers, be compassionate and humble." I like when a person shares something that God has done for them in a miracle or answer to prayer. It helps strengthen my faith that God can do ANYTHING TODAY!

I have heard people say they learn about God while out in nature. I love being out in nature and it makes me feel good, and peaceful, and forget all my problems and relax. I could just sit and watch any animals that are around or enjoy looking at the trees. I feel close to God there and you may too.

I talked about this already—don't judge your relationship with God just by your feelings! I've heard things like, "I get to know God in nature." OK, you learn that God can make beautiful things and places. Do you learn God's love for people there, do you learn that Jesus is the Son of God, do you learn God's patience, and God's healing power, His forgiving grace, and much more??? Notice you learn very little in nature. You get to know God by studying the Bible alone and in groups, prayer time, and quiet time.

I go to the church I do because I have things in common with these people. Probably very few people, or none, have the exact same beliefs I do but I feel comfortable sharing beliefs with these people. The people I worship with have a life style similar to mine. Some of them work at the same place I work. I want to worship with friends. Most have become friends since we started going there.

You have heard of people, and maybe you know someone who works with city gangs, for example. We probably would not share a common background with most of the congregation so I would not feel comfortable. The true and holy word of God may be taught there as well as in my church. They may do things differently than I would–but they may have a personal and righteous relationship with Jesus.

You also need to know that some "groups" or "churches" do not have the same basic core beliefs that we have. They may be bound closer than most church groups and they may appear to be filled with love but, they may not be as they appear. Even people that worship Satan may have a "pretty good" worship service and they may appear to love all people but they are a long way from our beliefs.

So I say to you, before you join a church group, study what you can and then talk to someone there—ask direct questions—test the things you see and hear against what the Bible teaches. Get an understanding of your group and some day someone may ask you what your church teaches.

The people we worship with have the same basic core beliefs about God and Jesus and the Holy Spirit that I have. Reverend Dean LaVelle our preacher, opens the Bible and then speaks. When we leave we know where the message came from.

People in our church are willing to be my support team and I'm sure they know I support and pray for them. Life is meant to be a team effort.

Let me change the subject a little and tell you a story. I was out on the flight line one day along with the crew of our largest aircraft firefighting truck, when a fighter plane radioed it was coming in with hydraulic problems. Sensors in the plane indicated that the nose wheel might not be down all the way and locked in place!!! Now let me explain—near the beginning of the runway a cable is kept across the runway for emergency use. "Donuts" along the cable hold it a few inches off the pavement.

On the bottom back of a fighter plane is a hook. If you hold out your arm and cup your hand facing downward–that is about the size of the hook. Easily speaking, that cable across the runway is spring loaded. The object is for the airplane hook to grab that cable just as the wheels hit the pavement. (These pilots are really good!) Well, just like in the movies—this time the hydraulics gave out and the front wheel system collapsed, the nose of the plane skidded across the pavement with flames racing up the sides of the aircraft. In no time at all the foam and water from our large fire fighting truck was on the plane and the flames were gone.

If you ever get a chance, ask that pilot how important the support team is to him!!!!! If you think about it, every preacher needs a support team. Every evangelist and every leader and every worker should have a support team. Every new Christian should have a mentor and/or support team. We're all in this airplane/family together and:

This is my Father's World!!!!

P.S. Christianity was never meant to be an "individual" program" but rather a team effort. "Put on the whole armor of God." Let's look at old movies–it always took one, sometimes two or three people to dress a soldier in armor. For Example, the big breast plate had to be one piece in front therefore it had to fasten in the back.

Every knight required assistance when putting on his suit of armor. Who are you helping to prepare themselves to go out and meet the world? Who is out there running around the world feeling more confident and secure because they know if the shoe string comes untied that you will always be available to help? (Try to tie your shoes in a suit of armor) if the chain link neck piece starts to come unhooked, will someone be there to help?

P.S. Carefully read Ephesians 6:11-20 and notice that we are to put on the <u>FULL</u> armor of God!!! NOT just part of it. For example, don't go out without the shield of FAITH or without being covered by the helmet of salvation. In other words, don't go out unless you are fully dressed.

Notes

My Memorial of Memories

CHAPTER 15

I'd like to share a story with you. At work we have several vehicle parking areas. The one I park in has many empty spaces when you get out away from the building. Once in awhile someone will ask me why I park way out there by myself and with no regard to the white lines. I will try to explain to you why I do that and why my favorite Bible story means so much to me.

I'll start this story after I got hurt and went through the surgery. I would go back for a doctor visit and he would ask about changing careers to a less physical job. I did not want to change jobs or even think about it.

Like I mentioned before, I had an excellent surgeon. But it made me quite nervous when he would say, "Have you decided what kind of career, or job, you want to go into?" I definitely did not want to change jobs and I could learn to be very careful and not hurt my neck any more—somehow.

Some of my doctor appointments would be fairly early in the morning so we would drive up there late night and stay in a hotel.

Then we could sleep a little later in the morning and get to the doctor refreshed.

Then one night we were asleep in the hotel and in the middle of the night the Holy Spirit woke me up!! No flashing lights or angel choir singing. Just all of a sudden I sit up in bed and I'm wide awake. He said "Pray for someone."And immediately I said, "Who do I pray for and what do I say?" A lady in our church came to mind. (Incidentally, I know she had been praying for my healing.) I prayed for a while that she would receive a special blessing that day and that all of her needs be met. Then I fell back to sleep.

A little later in the night the Holy Spirit woke me up again and said "Pray for someone." Again I asked, "Who do I pray for and what do I say?" My Sunday school teacher came to mind and I prayed that he would receive a special blessing that day and that all his needs would be met. Then I fell back asleep.

In the morning we got around and went to my doctor appointment. My doctor did not mention changing jobs that day or ever again. Well that morning I understood. I believe God was showing me that He would take care of me and that He was over my future—AND—I need to pray more and care more about the family of God around me!!! I do pray for people and visit people better now.

Sometimes I stop and say, "Why me, Lord? Why me?" Especially in the last few years it seemed that my God has singled me out and sent special blessings and answers to prayers to me and my family–and I know people that may be more deserving! I sometimes think of Abraham–he made some mistakes and was not counted as perfect but he was called the Father of Faith!

Sometimes I think of Moses—WOW!! Day dream a minute— How would you like to have walked up to Saddam Hussein (Moses went up to the Pharaoh of Egypt) and said "Let all the people go who want to leave in peace or God will send grasshoppers to eat all your food crops!"

You might be killed right there—or at the very least you would be laughed out of town. Would you like to know what I envy about people like Moses? Moses, Abraham and many others KNEW THE VOICE OF GOD!! Moses could have said, "You want me to tell the King of Egypt you will send grasshoppers? You're kidding. This is just a nightmare; no God would want me to tell a message like that." It thrills me and excites me greatly that this same God that took care of Moses is taking care and blessing me!!!! WHY ME, LORD?? I deserve nothing but God has cared for and blessed ME and our family!!

Now skip ahead a little while. I was off work several months longer than expected. When I did get to start back to work I was still extremely weak. I felt I was completely safe driving my small pick-up back to work. But it did tire me out—so I would enter the parking lot and think it was simplest if I just parked out by myself. If I was really exhausted, I did not even pay attention to the lines—wherever I stopped the pickup—that is where I parked.

As time went on I got stronger, but I continued to park the same way–anyway–out there by myself. In time I realized that when I came out to the pickup after work I'd get in the pickup and I'd realize how far I'd come physically since those days that I was not sure I'd be able to keep the job! Probably every day, I'd sit there a minute and say praises to God before and while I drove home.

Let me stop there in my story and tell you about my favorite Bible story. Joshua is taking the people into the Promised Land and the men carrying the ark are going first and as they stick their foot out into the river for that first step–their foot came down on dry ground!!! The river parted and all the people walked across.

You may say "so what, we've seen this done before when Moses led all the people out of Egypt." But wait, when Moses led the people they were running away. They were getting away from an incoming army that might kill them or at least take them back to slavery!!! They were running away from being slaves and all the physical pains of being slaves. They were running away from all the years of praying and asking God to help them and take them out of here! They were afraid of what these incoming soldiers would do. They were mad at Moses, confused, and mixed up about all that's going on.

But look at what is going on as Joshua led the people through the dry Jordan River bed. I see the people excited and talking about "the end of the desert trip" and going into the land of milk and honey. They are going into a better life. They are going into a permanent home where they can work the land and eat well. Yes they may have to fight off giants or whoever but I see the people as excited.

In all the excitement of coming to the end of years of desert travel God told them to have one person from each of the 12 tribes to pick up a rock from the middle of the river–FROM THE MIDDLE OF THEIR MIRACLE–God told them to take that rock with them as they came out of the river bed. Then God told them to make an altar that would stay there for generations to come.

For years and years that altar was there and whenever the people passed the children would ask "Daddy what is that pile of rocks" and that would be a reminder and an opportunity to pass the story down through the generations.

Now that you understand my favorite Bible story, you understand why I tell parents–start a scrapbook or something that will contain reminders of things that happen in your child's spiritual life. These reminders (pictures, notes, awards, etc.) will be reminders to your child and then to their children of the things God has done!

Now you can understand that in a way my pickup out there became my altar of memories. Most every day as I walk out to that pickup, I'm reminded that God helped me to heal and that HE helped me keep my job and my way of life. My God has shown me through all this time that:

This is my Father's World!!!!

P.S. One more "huge" little story. This is not directly related to the above–it is a small story that took a huge amount of determination. It takes a lot to get me to start something (I'm a very busy person already) but once I'm convinced God wants me to do something there is no stopping me!! I only tell you this to have you to be on constant alert—God may have you do odd things at odd times! Be alert and ready. You may or may not ever know why you did something. The task may be to grow in obedience that prepares me for later things—or I may be doing something that blesses or builds up the other people involved. When you believe God wants you to do something–DO IT. Here goes:

A long time ago there was a "situation" that happened that involved several people. Well, someone threw my name in and said I was involved. That was not true and I said some unkind things about that person. A few days later I believe God was telling me I had to go to that individual and apologize for saying those things! Needless to say, this individual was not on my list of people to send a valentine to every year. I also tried to tell myself that was not God talking to me. This was a terrible thing to have to do!! I don't do apologies very well. But God's ways are not easy ways–say that again–<u>God's ways are NOT easy ways!!</u> It took strength that I did not have but I apologized to that person for the things I said even though he was not there and may not know I had said these things. Why should I have to apologize?? It wasn't for him—it was for me. My obedience in doing what God says is most important and over everything.

I have a long way to go but I seek to learn to know the voice of God and I hope I never miss doing what I'm told; no matter how difficult it is.

If and when you feel God is telling you to do something–listen, pray, and think about it. If you are like me–I think God keeps me one step beyond what I am capable of!! (I don't know who gets all the easy jobs.)

Keep that notebook or binder and always write all these things in it. Answers and "why's" may come to you later.

This is my Father's World!!!!

Notes

Just Plain Luck

"...He causes His sun to rise on the evil and the good, and sends rain on the righteous and the unrighteous," Matthew 5:45.

Please read this carefully and understand what I'm saying. I see this while I am farming. One of my neighbors is not a Christian but when the rain comes it falls equally on my farm and his farm.

Now, please understand that God made the rain to happen automatically BUT He also has the power to change those laws or results anytime He wants. In Joshua 10:12-15, God had the sun stand still for several hours (about 12 hours) because Joshua asked. Since the day was longer, the battle continued and Israel was able to defeat the Amorites. In Mark 4:39, Jesus made the storm stop and the waves to be peaceful!! God created this earth and all the laws of nature and all the life upon the earth so he has all power over them.

God allows many things to happen by coincidence or chance or laws of nature or fate etc. Let's look at a few other things. God allows both the saved and the unsaved people to have a baby. For the most part the baby is a result of nature (heredity, DNA, the eye color and hair color, problems). Both the saved and the unsaved parents take a chance and they hope (some pray) that their child will be a beautiful, healthy, and a normal baby. REMEMBER THAT GOD CAN CHANGE ANYTHING HE WANTS TO!! For example, if the baby is born with problems God may or may not heal the baby's problems—God has the power of miracles—or the right to let things happen as they will!! God has promised to be with us and to help us through any and all situations but He didn't promise to change everything as we want it.

I hope you understand exactly what I mean. If a wall of flood water comes rushing at us–my unsaved neighbor's home and my home have equal chances that they will be destroyed by this act of nature. However, I have a prayer line straight to the God who created this earth and He can change the flood or protect my house or protect part of my things depending on my faith and God's reasons!!! Or God may allow my house to be totally destroyed. I may not know or understand those reasons.

My unsaved neighbor lives a life controlled by coincidence, chance, laws of nature, and fate or whatever. I live a life filled with miracles and answers to prayers, controlled by the very God that created this earth and all that's here. Things that are chance and laws of nature are a part of my life too but; I know my God is over them.

I have heard the saying, "I'll wait until I'm old and have lived a fun life then I'll become a Christian before I die." Or I've heard that, "You want to accept Jesus as your savior so you can go to heaven." I WANT YOU TO ALWAYS REMEMBER THAT GOD WILL HELP YOU LIVE HERE ON EARTH and then TAKE YOU TO HEAVEN!! God can and will work miracles and answers to prayer here on earth that will make life better for you!!

I believe God has worked lots of miracles or answers to prayers in my life that I did not notice or was not aware of—plus any miracles that I am aware of!! How does a person tell??The first thing is that your life must be truly and accurately aligned with

God's plan for you. You need to be walking and talking with God without ceasing. You need to be in God's plan for you and trying to live a holy life seven days a week. You can't be "more Christian" one day or another just as you can't be more American one day or another. You are either American or not.

Good luck! Yes, I believe in luck or chance but let me explain so you will understand what I mean. Remember that God created this world and all within. This is my father's world; He created it and He is over it all! When God created this world and everything in it—He also created what we call nature and the laws of nature. For example, God created gravity and laws of nature that deal with gravity. We all live by the laws of gravity—both Christians and the non-Christians—and gravity treats each one the same. If you fall out of tree there is only one direction you will go. That is the same direction I or anyone else will go also. Jesus felt this same gravity when He walked on the earth. Gravity held him down to the ground so he could walk or lie down or sit at the dining table without floating away and bouncing off the ceiling. Jesus lived on earth to experience the same things that we go through in life and I'm sure he experienced the laws of nature like we do.

However, since Jesus and God (Jesus was in the beginning (John 1:1-2) created the world, they have the ability to **control the laws as they wish.** That is how Jesus could walk on the water (Matthew 14:25-31) without the influence **of gravity pulling Him down.** That is also how God could hold back the water of the red sea for Moses so that all the people could cross to the other side. Jesus could tell the storm to calm down and he could walk on water. God and Jesus created this world and they have total power over everything, including nature!!

Now, if we agree on that let's go a little further. The Bible says it rains on the just and the unjust (Matthew 5:45). When they created the world they set many, many laws and acts of nature in motion. For example, they designed water so that it could evaporate into the atmosphere. Then when wind and temperature are just right the moisture forms into heavy drops and falls to the ground as rain.

I believe that God created these actions to be automatic–whenever these conditions are just right it will always result in rain. Since that is consistent the weather person is able to predict the weather with some degree of accuracy.

When the right things get to the exact correct balance the results will be raindrops falling on my head automatically. God does not have to form each little raindrop and then send it down to earth. **HOWEVER:** ALWAYS REMEMBER THAT: This is my Father's World!!!! And He has complete control over it!

Remember when Jesus was sleeping in the bottom of the boat and His disciples woke Him up because they were all going to die in the terrible storm. In my mind I can see Jesus calmly going out onto the front of the boat and thinking "My father and I created laws of nature that caused the rain to fall on them and the air temperatures that move the air around as winds–**THEREFORE** I have complete control over nature and can change any of it that I wish to change." In Mark 4:39 Jesus said, "Quiet! Be still!" And the severe storm completely stopped as quickly as Jesus could tell it to change!!

I want you to completely understand this. God created this universe where the right combination of events will automatically result in a predetermined outcome. For example, the rain will form when conditions are correct and it will fall on the believers and the non-believers. HOWEVER, we are children of the king: This is my Father's World and he is ALWAYS over the laws of nature and can change them as He desires. Remember in (I Kings 17:1) where Elijah prayed and it did not rain or when the sun stood still (Joshua 10:13). WE KNOW this mighty creator, this master of all nature, this King of kings and Lord of lords, this Jesus that came to the earth as a man, died on the cross to save each of us.

We know this mighty Creator, who can change nature and the results of nature according to His desire.

Another example, if I sit under an apple tree just as an apple falls out of the tree I might get hit on the head just by luck. I don't think God looks down and says "Hey look, there is James sitting under the apple tree. One of you angels run over there and throw an apple down and hit him on the head!" Sir Isaac Newton was not the first person to be hit by a falling apple. He may have been the first person to think of gravity when he got hit by the apple!

I sometimes refer to the things that I have no control over as good luck or bad luck or chance depending on whether I wanted these things to happen or not. If I wanted the rain, when it happened I might say that is good luck. Always keep in your mind that God is over everything and that He could change the weather whenever He wants and/or whenever we ask (If we have enough faith). This is what we call a miracle or answer to prayer!!

This is my Father's World!!!!

Notes

Throw Away World

CHAPTER 17

We actually do live on a throw-away world! This is a disposable earth that we live on. I've read that if you see something, it is of this world. If you cannot see it, it is of the spiritual world. God planned this universe and all that is in it. The earth has no value to God other than for us to live on. The land, oceans, the seas, and the skies were created just for us. The plants and animals of this world were made for us, Genesis 1:28-30.We are the ultimate creation and made in His image. He planned the very beginning and the final ending!! The days are numbered and only our God knows the number. Most problems of this earth are "pennies" to our God. We have a lot of disposable things we use in our daily lives. Our trash disposable systems are over loaded trying to remove "junk" and "garbage" as fast as we make it.

For example, a TV set has a purpose. We properly use it until it quits–then throw it in the trash and forget it. If a coffee pot quits, throw it away. If a car quits–we might fix it a few times–and then recycle it and trash the rest. Nothing worldly lasts forever and most only a few years.

Some people save up "treasures" like money and gold. They collect wealth and riches that will take them through any problems and give them a "great life" when they retire.

Some people "collect" land or kingdoms as they go through life. If I remember right, President Saddam Hussein of Iraq had numerous people killed to protect himself and to protect his position here on earth. He even had one of his sons killed to be sure his kingdom would survive and thrive. His "position" in this world was the most important thing in his life.

Let's go back earlier in history. I Samuel chapter15, King Saul did not follow God's instructions for the battle with the Amalekites. God was grieved He had made Saul king. Then God had Samuel anoint David as King, I Samuel chapter 16:13 (read the whole chapter). From that day on the Spirit of the Lord came upon David in power. King Saul loved his position as King too much. He became jealous and tried to kill David, but God prevented that from happening.

People go to tremendous extremes to protect or to build their earthly kingdoms! People have literally given up their "rights" into the eternal heaven to chase gold or empires of wealth and status or dreams of great worldly success. They traded their eternal soul for "fun" times on this earth. These worldly achievements will all be cast aside or thrown away AND completely forgotten and never remembered again the second you die!

Look at Matthew 21:33-40. The men that rented the vineyard have already killed and beaten some of the landowner's servants and in verse 38b they are plotting to kill the land owner's son to get his inheritance (land). This shows the extent some people will go to get ownership of land.

Let's look at Luke 12:16-21. This farmer has a really good crop– that is what farmers hope and pray for every year. Some years he may only have gotten enough to fill half of his grain bins. This year he got lots of grain and it sounds like he did not have enough storage room. To me it sounds like reasonable management to increase his storage capacity. God has truly blessed him this year!

But verse 19 sounds like he gives himself "credit" and then he says to himself, "Relax and live because I have done so well." God then said he was a fool for not recognizing and thanking God for all that he has. Anyone who thinks he has made himself a rich, self-centered life to rejoice in has taken the wrong road toward eternity. When we accept Jesus as our Savior and Leader, and praise God for <u>everything</u> we have–then we will have the chance to relax in heaven and eat at the big banquet table because:

This is my Father's World.

Remember, God reigns in heaven. That's a place, or a world, or a kingdom that God has built for His truly faithful people to dwell forever with Him. It's a place where wealth has no meaning because it is so common around you. A place where even the streets you walk on are made of gold (Rev. 21:21). Now let me stop there and think a little bit. Gold is a soft metal that wears really easy–yet it seems that in heaven it must be solidly enduring if we can walk on it but it never ever wears out. So the things of heaven (spiritually and physically) (not physically as we know it maybe) must be everlasting and stable. Therefore, there are no damaging earthquakes, no floods, no landslides–not even soil erosion washing away like it does on my wheat field here on earth! God made AND reigns AND waits for us to join HIM in a perfect AND everlasting place!! That is not like this earth which is (spiritually and physically) being destroyed around us. Some day God Himself will destroy this world or allow it to be destroyed. It is "pennies" to a God that lives in a heaven that I can barely, barely imagine even in my wildest dreams!!

When we lived in Europe in the military we did not use pennies. Everything was rounded off to nickels. I liked that– pennies take up more room than they are worth. When I first came back to the United States I thought pennies were a waste of space and I used to throw them on the floor of the pickup. Later I decided to keep those pennies that had a use or value for me and throw the others in a can. That is the way the world is—WE, OURSELVES, are the valuable silver dollars that our God will protect and keep AND the physical things and dreams of this world will be thrown away. YOU are the bright and shiny star that is worth more than all the riches of this world!! YOU are the reason that Jesus came down from that perfect heaven to walk and die and rise again in this disposable world.

This earth was made as a temporary living place for man. When God created this world, He made man to have dominion over everything on earth. Take care of all things responsibly. Don't hurt/kill/destroy anything needlessly. On the other hand man and animals are not equal. Jesus died for you and me. Genesis 3:21 says, "The Lord God made garments of skin for Adam and his wife and clothed them." This clearly shows that God used animals for the good of man. He made Man in his image with a spirit and a soul.

Don't ever doubt if THIS IS MY FATHER'S WORLD!! HE made this world, HE owns this world, HE has ultimate control over this world AND HE is so powerful and HIS kingdom is so great—that this world is merely the footstool where he can rest his feet if he ever decides too. But, HE chooses to love and protect and guide and nurture HIS precious followers until the day and the second HE chooses to dispose of this world and all the pain and suffering and destruction it contains. Yes:

This is my Father's World!!!!

Oh let me never forget!!!!!

Notes

Listen to God

CHAPTER 18

Parts of this book are from my past notes, and parts are of recent happening that I may not fully understand yet. It is written that God is the same yesterday, today, and tomorrow and I can believe that. However, I want you to understand that WHAT GOD DOES MAY VARY. I'm saying: don't think of God as a computer system!! Don't think, "When I get this particular problem—God will do this or that! Instead God's answer may differ by the exact circumstances and what is best. God has communicated with me a few times and in different ways and I pray He will communicate with you too.

I want you to understand that God works in various ways and you and I need to be alert. Pray without ceasing (1 Thessalonians 5:16) does NOT mean we walk around with our head bowed and hands folded but rather that we stay in tune to–or that we stay in harmony with our God so we will recognize what God does or says in our lives.

I've said several times that I believe God wants us to walk and talk with Him. We were created to live in the Garden and walk and talk daily with our God and Creator. By far my greatest problem is myself. Again I say, "**MY WORST ENEMY IS MYSELF**." When God does or says something in your life the temptation of doubt will start in on you quickly. You'll get thoughts like; maybe that was just me thinking it; I don't want to tell anyone and then get ridiculed, and am I sure I heard correctly?

1 Thessalonians 5:19 "Do not put out the Spirit's fire…" is very important. Don't do anything or say anything that would distract someone from "being on fire for Jesus." Never hurt someone's motivation for God. "I pray that the Holy Spirit will be in me as a raging fire that spreads fast and boils out from within me." Do not under estimate the power of the Holy Spirit. Do not ignore the Holy Spirit working in you. Do what the Holy Spirit says quickly, don't wait.

We need to align our heart and soul and mind with God. Part of (read it all please) Romans 8:5-8, "…those who live in accordance with the Spirit have their minds set on what the Spirit desires. … Those controlled by the sinful nature cannot please God." Romans 12:2 says, "… be transformed by the renewing of your mind. Then you will be able to test and approve what God's will is." "By the renewing of your mind", means that we are to think differently than the world thinks, if we want to get close to God. So we need to be "changed" from our worldly thinking. Col.3:2 "Set your minds on things above, not on earthly things."

Let me give an example: First let me try to explain something that sounds really simple but can make a difference. What you do and hear and see and say and think does affect your actions… Day dream with me a little. Let's say that Joel is leaving church some Sunday noon and someone says "God bless you this week Joel and May your Dad be with you through the week." That means 10-year-old Joel will be setting the standards of where they go and what they do and may his Dad follow him around this week! They are limited only by the fact Joel is too young to get into some businesses. We recognize Joel as the leader and most responsible when we say that sentence and decrease the role of 32-year-old Jason (Dad) to a lower person than Joel!!

Now let me stop and think a minute: we say, we hear, we even sing songs that do just that. It may be a little thing: BUT, it sets the "chain of authority" that may lead to our actions! We sometimes say, "God go with you," to people as they leave the church. This sets up a frame of mind that God will go with me wherever I go and follow me around. God will follow me around and never leave me but wouldn't it be better if I said, "Go with God and May He lead you and bless you this week. Let me explain better. If you are following someone–where are your eyes? (On them) If someone is following you–where are your eyes? (In the world—where you are going.)

Therefore, if you keep your eyes on my God, you will recognize Him as the superior all knowing leader. If you follow Him you will do and say the right things all week!! Your mind and heart and eyes will be on Him!!! You will be blessed!!! It starts out a little thing but it can become a big thing very quickly. So what we say and what we hear and what we do "aligns" our heart and soul and mind for the week!!

God has communicated with me and I pray you walk so closely with Him that you enjoy the wonderful excitement, joy, and peace of being close to and communicating with Him. Remember, God may vary things–in other words–God does not get boring!!!! Mostly I'm going to try to tell you what I think has happened in my life so you can be encouraged to walk closer to our God and KNOW that He wants to be close to us here on the earth He created just for us.

Talk often and listen a lot. Pray often—I often ask God to give me the words to say because I don't understand. You know the song "What a Friend we have in Jesus?" Do we mean it? Actually take a piece of paper and write down the characteristics of a friend—write exact things you look for in a close friend. Now look at the list. Do you treat Jesus like a friend? Do we talk to Jesus like a friend?

One of the big events in my life was chapter 3 when I saw Jason standing over his world and God was over Jason's world and the whole world. Our God is over everything!!!!!

Understand that when you hear, "God is the same yesterday, today, and tomorrow," that refers to God's "characteristic." By that I mean God has the same powerful love for us all the time. The Old Testament is a book about a nation or people that followed God, then didn't, then followed God, then didn't! However, through all this–God is the same–meaning He loved the people no matter what! It's very important you understand this.

I was getting hung up in guilt once and I thought God would not want to use me or work in me anymore. I thought I'd still be going to heaven—but God would not work through me: especially if my reputation was tainted.

Hold that thought a minute. Abraham is one of my many favorite people and other people often use him as an example too. In Romans 4:3, "Abraham believed God, and it was credited to him as righteousness." Also, Abraham is known as the father of faith.

I thought Abraham was almost perfect and did no wrong–he is the father of faith!!! He must have been something! I have often said that maybe the <u>greatest thing was that</u> <u>Abraham knew God's voice</u>!! He would not have put his son on the altar to sacrifice him if he was not 100% sure that was God talking to him!! I'd like to know God's voice that well. Sometimes I pray and listen, with all my might, because I want God to tell me something. But God does not always answer me in the way I want. I just realized something, while I am concentrating on what I want, God may be giving me the answer I want in some other way and I am missing it. I/We need to keep alert and ready for God to answer us.

But then some guilt crept into my head for some things I had done. Then one day God told me to read and look at Abraham's life. Abraham made some bad mistakes and God still called him the father of faith. Then I felt a peace that God would still work through me and still loved me. If God decides to work through me it is totally based on God's never ending power and never diminishing ability—and my total lack of ability!! Numbers 22:28 The Lord made the donkey talk to Balaam so I understand my excuses or lack of abilities are no real challenge for God!!

I used to think God would only answer prayers that were along the line of His will and work. But now I also believe that God sometimes answers prayers that are just a favor because He loves me. Also I believe God talks to me or answers prayers to teach me something or just for the experience to build confidence. I told you in chapter 13 about our waitress with the pulled tendons in her ankle.

Things like that are happening more often to teach me to be BOLD! Do not worry about what other people will think—Be Bold—stand out—and do what God wants you to do.

God works in different ways!! But my story starts with a simple test. (Don't start with a super major life threatening situation because you must learn to keep an open mind that can/will accept ANY ANSWER...) Maybe 20 years ago, there was a lot of talk about the state death penalty. I knew what the state should do and I voiced my opinion with friends. Later I felt I should ask God about this. I knew what the state should do but I am confident I kept an open mind for the answer and I prayed and ask God what He says. This was a new experience for me!! I felt that it was a test–I tried with all my heart to not prejudge and that I promised to accept the answer totally–even if it went against what I believed. (Much later: the truth may have been that God put that subject on my mind so I could learn from this subject that was not really close to my heart.)

I felt God gave me an answer to what He says about the state death penalty and I had to accept that answer. NOTE: Do NOT ask if you are not willing to live with the answer!! This whole "test" was something I had no power over nor was it an earth shaking "need to know." But, I believe God used this experience to excite me and make me want to walk closer with Him. Take time to talk with God, ask questions, share feelings, and be willing to accept whatever answer we get. At the end of our prayers don't we say something like, "... thy will be done on earth" Mean it or don't say it!!

Often times God will wake me in the middle of the night to write. Here is a slightly different example. Susan and our youngest daughter, Erin, sometimes sing in church—it is a wonderful story how God has given them songs and a real excitement to sing. Well it was the time of year when people were getting ready for Christmas and church programs. I remember one night in particular that I was praying about, "Father God, I just thank you so much for saving me and taking care of me and I know I owe you everything. I'd like to do something for you–not because I have to–but because I want to. Susan sings wonderful and she sings with such love and excitement and there isn't anything I am doing like that right now. Please let me do something."

Well, Christmas passed and I got busy with life. I worked second shift and I'd get home about midnight. I was really busy with the job in town, farming chores, and working on farm machinery trying to get things ready to operate for the summer. I'd heard our church was to have an Easter program and Susan was one of the people to sing. But I was so busy on the farm that I didn't pay much attention.

Six nights before the church program I got home about midnight and like usual I can't go right to sleep so I started to play solitaire on the computer.

Then I felt like God was going to have me write. I've learned that even if I'm asleep and I feel this way I need to get up and get a pen and paper!! If I don't get to writing, the information will be lost. It is not usually repeated. So I started writing but this time was a little different and I was wondering where this was taking me—just then my mind stopped writing and I saw myself knelt down and praying and I could hear myself saying something like, "Father God, I just thank you so much for saving me and taking care of me and I know I owe you everything. I'd like to do something for you–not because I have to–but because I want to. Susan sings wonderful and she sings with such love and excitement and there isn't anything I do like that. Please let me do something." Nothing was said about what was happening but instantly I understood that now was the answer to that prayer a few months before. I'd guess this whole answer to a prayer, from a few months earlier, took a second and I understood and a deep peace came over me and then I was back to writing. I wrote some that night, the ideas stopped and I went to bed and sleep. The next night the same thing happened and I got the rest of the story!

The Easter activity bulletins were already made but they let me in. I wore a robe and told a story of how I was a traveling sales person in Jerusalem and throughout all the country and I sometimes heard stories of a Jesus. I caught up with Jesus on the way to the cross as Susan sang "Were You There." People said it was really good and I told them that the amazing story started a few days before.

I have already told you that about 20 years ago I became a lay speaker (that means I do not have a formal education degree in the Bible) or guest speaker. I was working out in the yard one afternoon. Susan had taken the kids out to Wichita, Kansas and I was just getting a few things done. In my mind I saw that silly old thing that some people talk about—I saw me up in tree sawing off a branch BUT I'm on the wrong side of the saw! Well that was silly so I just kept working. I saw that again in my mind and somehow I realized that my God had something I was supposed to do and it involved speaking to groups of people. It did not require special training–just forget my past and step out in complete faith–trusting God to take care of me wherever I go.

"Wherever I go" struck a tender nerve and I began to argue. I would go anywhere as long as I don't have to fly—I don't want to fly anywhere. I remember thinking "I can be honest with God—He already knows everything." I would go anywhere I could drive. After a little communication I agreed I'd try to go anywhere. I got the understanding that God will give me the ability to do what is needed.

I said—there is nothing I can say that proves God is real or that Jesus took my sins away. I could show some things God has done (creation etc.) and I could tell some things that I believe God has done–but I don't think I can say anything that would make an atheist or non-believer become a Christian.

After a little while God said, "You just say what I give you to say–it is the Holy Spirit's job to open their heart and convict them of sin and give them understanding."

I was nervous about writing sermons—example, if I tell about the Easter story one year what do I tell in years after that??

I don't have time!! I'm a full time student, have a long drive to school, husband, parent, and always busy.

My final argument was the fact that I didn't even have a suit to wear–and everyone knows that a speaker wears a suit and I couldn't get up in front of people without a suit to wear. (At that time in our lives we didn't have much money.)

About then the afternoon was over and Susan and the kids drove in. I wasn't committing myself to make a decision so I put it all out of my head and I went over and welcomed the family home. Susan had no idea what was going through me that day. She also knew that I would NOT spend money on clothes for myself. Susan had bought a second hand suit that was in excellent condition for only $5.00!! Five dollars! I just stood there and got tears in my eyes—I instantly knew the discussion was over and I was a lay speaker in the church.

That afternoon is such a beautiful story, I was stressed but God took that stress—one part at a time—and turned the stress into peace!! God did not "make" me do anything—He led me through my stress and fears and let me know He would always lead me. Like the Israelites he led me through the parted Red Sea, He took my fears and stress away as he provided a path. He personally led me through the Red Sea with all my worldly fears and excuses roaring high above me on both sides. He slowly and gradually gave me peace and a strong desire and confidence to do his will.

Sometimes God would wake me in the middle of the night. I'd be wide-awake (almost always) and I'd know to get up and write. I would see myself speaking from the podium and the congregation would be listening. I would write down what I was saying and even note some of the physical things I would do. This would take more than one night and basically when I would stop talking I would stop writing!! THEN–THEN I would start practicing and learning it. THEN–get this now–THEN I WOULD BE ASKED TO SPEAK SOMEWHERE !!! You know what???The second year the Easter or Christmas sermons were completely different than the first year!! I was amazed at how the same Bible story had different things come out of it each year!! Then it all stopped and we moved away to mid Kansas. God has not told me to do those things again.

There were other changes that were not visible. The main one was that I don't like to read–but during this time I really enjoyed (and looked forward to) reading the Bible and related books. This was really a big change!

Instead of speaking, God has me writing—this is to each one of you. YOU/each one of YOU is to read and then pray to the Holy Spirit for understanding. Each one of you will get some different understandings according to YOUR PERSONAL experiences and needs and most of all according to your relationship with Jesus.

Life is a trip, but you don't know where you are going because we don't know the future. (Death is different—you do know where you are going.) Life is about making the most of the trip. Let's just say you have a million hours to live. A third of that may be sleep time so I guess you could take all those hours out. I guess "life" is what you do in the rest of those hours. How is your "life" time going? The Bible says we are in this world but not of this world. That can cause kayos and stress. However, we know that God made the heaven and the earth so He knows everything about them. We also know that God created a man and a woman and that continued, as God even knew us before we were born!! We know that the Trinity will always be with us with unlimited power, wisdom and knowledge. Our creator is now within us.

Well OK, I admit I rarely stop and ask directions when I am driving. But I waste time. Wouldn't it make sense to have a guide? When you come to a fork and there are two ways to go and they both look interesting. Wouldn't it make sense to have a guide? When the world ends there is a banquet feast and my name card is sitting there above the plate! Wouldn't it make sense to have a guide? Someday, and maybe soon, Jesus is coming to get all of HIS true followers and this world will end. Wouldn't it make sense to have a guide? But wait: the creator of all things and master of all knowledge is within me. To enjoy the trip we call life, we need to make a definite effort to seek and search and study to learn to get closer to God and His ways and make HIM our guide!

Another event I'd like to tell you about happened while I was going to college (later in life). My major was technology education and I spent most of my time in the technology and materials rooms/labs. Dr. Illey was my main teacher and advisor part of the time. To set the background for this–one of our daughters was having problems; Susan was working at this time on a different shift than I lived on. (Especially young couples–don't work different shifts if at all possible!! We did not take the time to be together long enough to finish our fights!!)

(What's about me and fights??? A few times in my life we didn't get an argument resolved. I'd go around mad for a while or a few days. I'd think bad thoughts about her. I'd make sure she knew I was mad. That is not good! You all don't know my wife very well!! She gets terrible, Historical, mean and cruel!!! We have to get our differences resolved and then a big hug. Then I can go back to "life".) (Susan says, "That is ridiculous—we don't fight!!!" We do too fight—as much as I am going to!! OK we agree to differ—hug, hug—now back to the book.)

I made good grades but at times I got really stressed when I couldn't keep up my homework. About this time I saw the vision of Jason over his world and God over it all.

Dr. Illey had a small computer room we could use; so, one morning I went early to do some computer homework. While I was there Dr. Illey came into the neighboring room (shop) and did a little cleaning and just odds and ends. I had never seen this area without several people in it. He came over and started to visit. Remember I'm stressed so tight my rubber band is about to bust. (I would never have talked if someone else was around.) Well, I "let it all out" and he seemed to care. He shared something from his life and he prayed! This was a big thing in my life and I often share this story with people.

Look at this story. At first I was really too stressed to study much. I got to school early and into an empty computer room (empty computer rooms were rare). Doc came in and seemed to do a little but not real busy (Dr. Illey was never not busy— he was involved in many things AND was a loving/caring/ involved family man.) He came over to me. He listened and gave me someone to talk it out with. Sometimes I need someone to let me talk things out. (The Bible says to share, care, and pray to encourage one another.) Then he shared something from his life. (This was awesome!!) That put him on the same level as me, his life had problems too AND he trusted me enough to tell me!!! Also this gave me someone to pray for and helped get MY mind off MY world and MY problems alone. He prayed (I'm thinking that great men pray and know where the greatness comes from). I felt a peace and a true thankfulness.

That morning with Dr. Illey moved my prayer life to a new level!!! I had a list, and still do, of people I would read during my prayer time. I don't think I'd had a real prayer partner (other than Susan) that I opened up and really talked with. But it was more—I found myself really caring about his situation. I spent less time praying and thinking/worrying about my situation and more time during the day praying and caring about him and his family.

I think God blessed me and gave me peace better/sooner than would have happened as I learned to care. Remember years later in the night at the hotel, the Holy Spirit was teaching me to pray and care for others. Here again God was trying to teach me to care and pray and He will give me peace. I can see clearly how God worked through this man to teach me what it meant to be a prayer partner!! I will always thank Dr. Illey for accepting that "mission" on that morning!

One of the main prayers I say is, "Thank you Father God for the people you put around me!! You send people to encourage me, to care, to talk with me, to witness to me, to pray with me and more!!

I tell this story to people as a "bloom where you grow" and a whole lot more. I was telling this to someone lately and all of sudden I stopped and this news flash went through my mind "I put him there for you, James."

As I sit here writing, I get tears in my eyes—God has been so very good to me—I don't know why!!! I have a wonderful wife who gets her "spouse" training from the Bible. Not many people can really say that. There are Susan and I, six kids, and 34 grandkids–and we are basically all healthy!! Most likely we'll all worship God on Sunday mornings: we are so blest!!! I could never do enough to repay all my blessings!!

Remember this story, think about this story—are you ready to be on both sides of the story!!! If you haven't already—you will find people that need someone to listen and care. Share some of your own life with them. Share something that God has done in your life!!! Look around and see that God is alive and working today—if we will let HIM... Go BOLDLY and remember the curtain was torn from top to the bottom and WE can now go into the HOLY OF HOLIES AREA!! God can communicate with us and us with Him!! Remember, if you are following Jesus—YOU ARE PROPABLY OUT OF YOUR COMFORT ZONE and LOVING IT! If you get a chance, be a mentor to a new Christian and watch them grow! If you get a mentor use this opportunity to grow and remember:

This is my Father's World!!!!

Notes

Do Not Take God's Name In Vain

CHAPTER 19

I want to remind you to always remember–you belong to the greatest, most powerful, most loving, longest running, forever enduring, family the universe will ever know!! You are walking through life beside the Jesus who told the storm and wind to be still—and they did!! You have given your life and heart to the very God who created this world–AND–all the universe and galaxies around it!!!

There is absolutely no need too big that this Jehovah God cannot do!!!! I can tell you without any doubts that this God that we recognize as master over all gods has answered many prayers and done many miracles. Normally, I think answers to prayer and miracles are identified as such when they happen. However, I am sure there are many we fail to see, as He and His angels walk with us!!!

I want you to remember we serve a Jesus so loving and so powerful that He even brought Lazarus back from the grave. We serve a Jesus so caring that he served the fish and bread to the

5,000 people so they would not go away hungry and so gentle that he told His disciples to relax and let the children come sit around Him and talk to Him.

We serve a Jesus so "all knowing" that when He met the woman at the well He was able to tell her all about her life and He can do that with each of us!!

I want you to remember that no world government or no fighting armies or no politicians on on earth will ever have the power to stand upright before Jesus when He comes back to this earth to collect His followers!!!

Having understood that, I want you to write this on your brain and in your heart, "Do not take the name of the Lord your God in vain." As you get to know me you will realize that I do not easily fall to the temptation of using profanity. I want that command to mean much more to you than just God's name in profanity—it means don't take the name of God or Jesus unless you are going to believe, live in faith and allow God to be your guide and protection always. I want you to never take the name of Jesus lightly!!! I want you to ALWAYS walk tough and walk strong because you walk beside the KING of heaven and earth!!!!! I want you to walk in love and total submission and know that God is God.

"Do not take the name of the Lord your God in vain." When you say, "Jesus, I want to walk through life with you," mean it with all your heart and soul and mind and strength and do not vary away from that during good times or bad times!! We pray "in Jesus' name" because that name is the ultimate power forever and ever!!! When you say you will follow Jesus don't look back and don't look to the sides–keep your eyes on Him in the good times and the bad times.

This is like when Gma and I got married—she took my name. Gma Susan did not take my name "Mills" lightly or think that she could come and go; or that taking my name was something easy and didn't mean much. With my name she took on a whole new way of life different than she had been living. She accepted and took new responsibilities, new goals, and new problems. Gma Susan did not take my name in vain–she took it and then gave what was required and needed from her. She "wears" my name daily and lives accordingly.

I pray and pray that you will understand this and strive with dedication to live it. Sometimes when things are going good I like to sing songs like "In the Garden" and "I love thee Lord Jesus" and I feel close to Jesus as my friend and savior. But then when things get bad and tough I may forget all about Jesus and I get all stressed out and worried and I make more mistakes. So you see when that happens I had taken the name of Jesus in vain and when the going got tough I did not always trust Jesus enough to take care of my problems. Sometimes I claimed to be a Christian and walking with God but when I had a problem I failed to ask God to lead me through the problem when earlier I proclaimed that my God had the power to create this world and all the life on it. So earlier I had taken God's name in vain because I did not use Him when I could/should have done so.

So as I said in the beginning of this chapter, God is all–powerful, so take the name of Jesus and talk to Him in EVERY situation.

If I am to believe that Jesus loved me enough that he went through the beating—

If I am to believe that Jesus loved me enough that he suffered rejection, Mockery and denial as He died on the cross—

If I am to believe that Jesus loved me enough to go to the cross to save me—

Then I have to believe that Jesus is with me, cares about me, will lead me and protect me the rest of my life!! Don't take God's name casually.

"He didn't bring us this far to leave us."

Thou shalt not take the name of the Lord thy God in vain. Judas walked and talked with Jesus and saw the miracles for 3 years—but he was not going to follow God's will and plan. He had taken the name of Jesus but did not make Jesus the center of his life. Paul did not take the name of Jesus in vain. Paul knew that he walked with the power of an eternal all-powerful God. He called God to take care of him. Our God is all power. Our God is all love. Our God wants the best for us–He created the Garden of Eden as a perfect place for us to live. We messed that perfect plan up and lost the rights to that garden here on earth. Proverbs 9:10 tells us that, "The fear of the Lord is the beginning of wisdom, and knowledge of the Holy One is understanding." Proverbs 16:6 says, "Through love and faithfulness, sin is atoned for; through the fear of the Lord a man avoids evil." Can there be both—love and fear—there has to be both.

I sometimes use an example of a huge iceberg. I've seen pictures where a cruise boat drives up close to an iceberg. I would never go–the boat looks so small, so insignificant, and so totally helpless. The iceberg looks so much larger, so much more powerful, so overwhelming, and so scary. If a chip of the ice breaks off (nobody knows when or how much) and lands on the boat if will be destroyed and sunk. Or if a chunk of the ice breaks off and splashes into the ocean; that splash could sink the boat!!?? So I look at the pictures and I have fear so bad that I don't care to go. But at the same time, I will look at these pictures in awe and talk about how magnificently beautiful these icebergs are and how I would enjoy seeing them. It's the same with God. The Bible says God is all power!! He could have electricity jump out of a wall socket and kill me! He could have a large boulder fall on me when I visit the Rockies, or He could stop my next breath. In my life I've done some terrible sins against God. I now fear (have very strong respect and reverence) for God because I know He has the power to easily judge me and drop a rock on me, etc,—like that ice berg; God's power could as easily end my life the same as He was able to create a huge universe and this world and everything on it. I also stand in awe as I see the wonderful things God does, the time I held our first baby in the delivery room or when my first baby colt was born! Our God is truly a loving God who made a companion for Adam and I believe our God smiles at weddings to see the expression of "love" that He created in us. I worship a God so omnipotent, so caring that He sent His Son, Jesus, into the world to be my friend, my savior, my guide, my cornerstone and much more. Our God is everything, "I AM WHO I AM."

When you take the name of Jesus as your savior–mean it– recognize what His entire name includes–accept the responsibility, His love, and His almighty power. Don't take His name in vain– stand on it!!

This is my Father's World!!!!

Notes

Mini Lessons

CHAPTER 20

Nothing New

One of the things I like about living on the farm is that I can make piles of brush and burn them when I want. Occasionally a storm, or wind, or old age will cause tree limbs to fall—and we have a lot of trees. Usually I will pick these up in my spare time. I have a place I pile them and the pile gets bigger and bigger. When the grand kids are around we burn the pile and roast hot dogs and our favorite thing is making smoors.

After eating, some of us may sit and study the fire. If I remember my younger days correctly our science teacher said that we cannot create matter and we cannot destroy matter. The same goes for energy—we cannot destroy or create energy. I am reminded of that as I watch the tree branches being "destroyed." Actually, nothing is being destroyed or lost—the fire is merely rearranging the atoms of one material into the atoms that will consolidate to form molecules of another material.

For example, the branches will have some moisture or water in them. As the branch warms up the water is boiled out of the wood. This water is broken down and dissipated into the atmosphere.

It is not carelessly converted into gasses—as it may appear! It is precisely converted! Many molecules of water/liquid will be changed into many molecules of water/gas which is humidity!! This is done an immeasurable number of times every minute that I sit and watch the fire, yet each little molecule of water gets the exact process!!

If we look at the same fire with our attention on the energy involved, we will basically see the same type of action. Let's look at heat energy. When we look at heat energy we can measure the amount of heat in BTU's. If we boil water on the kitchen stove it will take a certain amount of energy to boil water. If we could measure the BTU's of heat given off by our fire we might be surprised. Some people believe that the heat energy in the wood, being converted to heat energy (all the heat sources in the world together) in the atmosphere is actually heating the earth's climate.

Now, I told you all of that so that you will understand: God took all that into consideration when He created the world and universe and beyond!!! He created the right number of atoms and all that stuff so the world and nature would be balanced and in harmony.

Also, I'd like you to realize that some of the simple basic principles or laws of nature that God created in this world have taken man thousands of years to figure out!! Also realize that God made all of this—everything you see and much more that we can't see! <u>Man cannot make even one atom!!</u> Man has been on this earth a long time and we cannot make even one part of an atom! Man cannot create anything. We simply rearrange atoms and molecules and elements into something different as we see fit.

The amazing part—the truly amazing part is that GOD SPOKE and EVERYTHING JUST APPEARED!!!!!!! God did not have bulldozers and cement trucks or hammers and nails!!! I think He just said the word like "waterfall" and there appeared a large beautiful waterfall with all the right atoms and molecules.

If you look a little further—dust to dust—our physical body, matter we are made of, will be changed but never destroyed when we die. Adam was made from the dust of this earth to which IT returned—my body will return to that dust as well.

Then there is only one thing left to discuss. If I believe, AND I do believe, God created us spiritually in His image. THEN I have a spirit or soul, of energy that cannot be destroyed or created—So it must live on forever and ever. That is eternal life—somewhere. I know that my "somewhere" will be in heaven with Jesus.

Pythagorean Theorem

We are going to look at a couple truths that will always work and you can always trust as you go through your lives.

We are going to learn how to build a building and get it square. You have heard the story about the man who built his house upon a rock and the storms came and the house survived because it was built upon the rock. Another man built his house on the sand and the storms came and the house washed away and fell apart and did not survive.

Well let's look at how to build a good strong "square" house because the guy that made his house on the sand may not have made his house very strong and because of that it fell down too easily.

When we build a house we have to build the walls very strong. If we build an outside wall it has to hold up the roof and a second story floor, if there is one. So a wall has to be made strong.

But, a corner has to be even stronger because it is where two walls come together—the corner has to hold the weight of the two walls and the corner has to lock the two walls together. So, the corner is a very important part.

Also the first corner is the most important because it makes all the rest of the house square! If the main corner is not square the others can't be square. I'd build from that corner.

To make that main corner square, we have a truth that will always work. It's called the Pythagorean Theorem. Here's how it works using simple measurements and very simple numbers. Start at the very important one and only, true starting point, corner stone and measure 4 feet along one wall and mark that point. Then measure 3 feet out on the other wall and make a mark. Now measure between the two marks; this is about math and algebra and why you go to school!

Now to keep things easy to understand, mark one of the two walls as "A" and the other as "B." Now mark the third side of the triangle as "C." Now let's roll some numbers using the formula...

1. "A^2"+"B^2" = "C^2"
2. $3^2 + 4^2 = C^2$
3. $9' + 16' = 25'.$
4. "C" = 5' (sq. root of 25)

The length of that third side measured between the 2 marks should be 5 feet!

I'll need your help to show what this means in real life. (Let's have a big person stand here and be the corner.) Some of you can stand with him/her so that "cornerstone" is marked very well. Remember, 3, 4, & 5. Then I'll measure out this way four feet and some of you stand here and mark this wall. Then I'll measure out this way from the corner three feet and some of you stand here and mark where this wall will be.

Now, stand there while I think... 4^2 is 16 and 3^2 equals 9. Then, $16 + 9 = 25$ and the square root of 25 is 5 feet. So! I measure between your two walls at exactly 4' and 3,' I will measure a distance of 5'. When the corner is exactly square, it will be ready to support and align the house walls. That is the Pythagorean Theorem. It is always truth and you can trust it if you build a house or anything else. You do not have to use the 3, 4, and 5 numbers; but, they are the easiest to remember.

Let's go back to the corner. Remember I said the corner had to be stronger to hold weight as part of two walls? So it needs to be made of something really strong. I'd say if you could make your corner out of really solid rock it would always be true and hold up.

Well, did you know the Bible talks about these things? God said in Isaiah 28:16 (read the whole chapter or at least verses 16-22) "Therefore thus saith the Lord GOD, Behold, I lay in Zion for a foundation a stone, a tried stone, a precious corner stone, a sure foundation: he that believeth shall not make haste." Jesus is the tried, precious, sure foundation, cornerstone that the church is built upon. Jesus is the cornerstone that my life should be built upon!

That is the Pythagorean Theorem. It is always true and you can trust it if you build a house or align your life.

He sent Jesus. Jesus is "the corner stone" that the people and the nation can build upon, because He is total truth and much more.

If we line up everything we do with Jesus, our lives will be true and straight and righteous. For example, if people are spreading a lie about another person, do you think that would be true and straight and righteous based on what Jesus did?

Or, if you have a chance to steal or rob from someone; how does that line up with Jesus, the cornerstone of our lives??

If we line up everything we do, with Jesus, our lives will be true and straight and righteous. As you go through life, check the things you say and do against Jesus. He is the true corner stone that we align our lives with. Don't let anything from this world get between you and the cornerstone. He is the solid rock—He can hold the weight of everything and anything that happens to you in this world! He is trustworthy—He walked this earth and knows everything that could possibly happen to you. Jesus is my Savior.

Tree Rings

How many of you have been to California and seen the huge Redwood trees? Closer to home; how many of you like to climb trees? How many of you have heard the story of George Washington cutting down the tree?

The story goes that he was asked about the tree and George said, "I cannot tell a lie. I cut down the cherry tree." The story doesn't tell why he cut down the tree; but I think maybe he did it so he could count the number of rings in the trunk of the tree.

I just happened to have a piece of a tree here with me. Can we find out how old this tree is? When we count the rings we know how old the tree is because each ring is a year. This tree has __ rings so it is ___ years old.

So I think maybe George cut down that cherry tree because he wanted to see how old it was. George Washington knew even more about trees. He probably knew that the tree grows more some years than other years. In other words, when the weather is good, the tree grows more that year, so the rings are further apart.

Let me make sure we all understand this. Each ring is for each year the tree has lived. The distance between the rings shows how much the tree grew that year.

If we were to write the year on each ring, starting with 2009 and going backwards, we could see the years that the weather was good and it rained just right and the tree grew a lot. Then we could ask someone like Clifford or Larry or Dean if those were the good years for growing things. (We would ask those guys because they have a lot of rings inside their trunk and they are probably as old as my piece of tree trunk here.)

Sometimes I think people are a lot like trees. People have good years that we learn a lot about Jesus and God and build a closer relationship with them. Sometimes we make bad choices and we don't grow like good Christians.

Maybe if we could look inside of your heart we could see how good a life you have lived. We could see the good growing years and the years we just don't grow as much. But we can't look inside your heart can we?

But God can. God can look in our hearts and see if we are having good days or bad days, and if we are growing as Christians. Let's read our Bible every day and pray we'll have good days and good years as we grow and learn to be good Christians.

We want to grow a lot, with Jesus, every day and year. Remember:

This is my Father's World!!!!

PS

I just realized something else about the tree's growth rings—the tree always grows a positive amount each year. In other words, a tree cannot "NOT" grow, every year the tree is alive there will be some space in the rings showing that the tree is growing.

Physically, if you are a child, normally speaking, you are growing a noticeable amount and getting taller every year. You can't change that, it just happens, just like the tree grows naturally.

Spiritually, it's the same way with us, every year that we are alive and living with Jesus—there will be a positive amount of growth. When we sin and ask God to forgive us, He removes that negative sin forever. So if we could see the growth ring in ourselves they would always be a positive noticeable amount of growth every year.

Jeremiah 31:34 "and they shall teach no more every man his neighbor, and every man his brother, saying, know Jehovah; for they shall all know me, from the least of them unto the greatest of them, saith Jehovah: <u>for I will forgive their iniquity, and their sin will I remember no more."</u>

Ps 103:12 "As far as the east is from the west, so far hath he removed our transgressions from us."